PRAISE

SUCCEED AS AN INC.

"Concise, insightful and action-oriented. T   ..eds a light on your blind spots and shows you clearly the baby-steps you can take every day, wherever you are, to create an inclusive culture. You'll find the keys to truly understand and manage human differences. A must-read for all managers of the 21st Century."

Chantal Goossens, Global Customer Director
THE COCA-COLA COMPANY

"Do you want to become the leader everyone wants to work with? Or simply a better citizen in the world? Then you must read Thais's book. I could not stop reading it. You'll find simple and powerful tools, such as the Propeller Model© used to check our blind spots and a great self-assessment tool. In part 2 we dive into different diversity dimensions with lots of examples."

Alberto Platz, Vice President Global Talent Acquisition and
Engagement
SWAROVSKI

"Thais is a true expert and professional of diversity and inclusion, being herself at the crossroad of different cultures and having dedicated most of her professional life to this essential matter. She is truly convinced, genuine, and authentic, and her book is a major contribution which will prove to be extremely useful to so many senior executives."

Edouard-Malo Henry, Group Head of Human Resources
SOCIÉTÉ GÉNÉRALE

"I believe a triple win (you win, the others win, and our society wins) comes true when you apply the values proposition in this book, a real philosopher's stone for our mind. Energising and transformational, this excellent-reading is a luminous arc taking you many levels upper in the way you see differences, in others and in yourself. As we are all wanderers in the incompleteness of life (Gödel's theorems), these pages empower you to build and share a self-transcendence improvement of our world using what we have all most in common, the strength of our incompleteness as human beings."

Marc Leymonerie, Group Director of IT Security Solutions and
Compliancy
AIR FRANCE KLM

"As a leader of global diversity and inclusion, the insight and perspective that this book offers around inclusive leadership is invaluable, to say the least. Thais Compoint's knowledge and expertise provides a very credible and unique approach to everything from building self-awareness to successfully motivating and engaging diverse teams. At Sodexo, our research pertaining to gender balance indicates that gender balanced teams perform at higher levels, are more engaged and have higher client retention, than those that are not. That being said, I have found this book to be a terrific reinforcement of these findings and others, as well as a great resource for uncovering additional ways to lead more inclusively."

Rohini Anand, Senior Vice President Corporate Responsibility &
Global Chief Diversity Officer
SODEXO

"Clear, enthusiastic, pragmatic, based on real life experiences, a much-needed tool box for anyone wishing to get going and to take profit of the value of difference."

Inès Duval, Diversity Director
SUEZ

"Thais tackles all diversity dimensions from a leadership perspective, focusing on the development of an inclusive culture that leads to greater business performance. This book addresses this beautiful topic in a very concrete way. It's packed with practical tools that you can apply to create a best in class diverse and inclusive workplace."

Véronique Vuillod, Vice President Human Resources France
COCA-COLA EUROPEAN PARTNERS

"A must-read for all managers of the 21st Century, who need to surf the wave of the globalised, cross-cultural and cross-generational workplace, and who want to boost team performance and innovation. Thais Compoint gives all the practical tips to find talent where it is: already surrounding us."

Géraldine Vallejo, Sustainability Programme Director
KERING

"A pragmatic approach for managers enabling the diversity of our world to translate into inclusion in XXI Century workplaces."

Tanguy de Belair, Diversity Director
VINCI

"Practical and easy to read; this book inspires you to think and act differently. Thais has gone to great lengths to share thought-provoking research and her experience in a well laid out book that I will be going back to time and again!"

Johanna Dickinson, Human Resources Director
KP SNACKS

"Thais simplifies highly complex diversity and inclusion topics, making them accessible to non-experts while empowering diversity and inclusion practitioners to make change happen. This book makes you feel good and get down to action straight away."

Stéphanie Oueda, Associate Director Diversity and Inclusion
COCA-COLA EUROPEAN PARTNERS

"This is an excellent introduction to the important topic of inclusive leadership. If you follow the themes of the book, it will transform your leadership style and take your team engagement to another level."

Sunil Sehgal, Senior Group Legal Counsel
BELRON INTERNATIONAL

"Thaïs has nailed the approach to Diversity & Inclusion in a clear and pragmatic way. Her book goes beyond the usual clichés and proposes simple steps for managers to become genuine inclusive leaders. You will discover that the recommended incisive steps are also highly relevant to your personal and everyday life. Don't miss this gem; it is unlike any other business books; it is spot on and life-changing.

Sylvain Guyoton, Vice President of Research
ECOVADIS

"A vivid presentation of inclusive leadership as a business growth driver, with a wealth of illustrative examples drawn from real-life. Reading this book just makes you feel like putting inclusion into practice, whatever your position, for the benefit of your team, your company and most importantly for yourself."

Ahmed Belaidi, Sales Manager France
HARRIS

"This is the perfect read for future leaders like me, who want to build a better world where people feel free to be themselves. Thais's book is an incredibly enlightening toolbox that empowers you to adopt a business leadership style at the service of people and society."

Sofia Greve, Business School Student
FEDERAL UNIVERSITY OF BAHIA

"Thais Compoint offers in her book not just her vision and knowledge of a highly experienced and qualified professional in the corporate world, but the vision and philosophy of a human who's sensitiveness and empathy draws the possibility of a fairer and enriching world. What a fantastic combination!"

Julia Evangelista, Founder
SEETHROUGH THEATRE COMPANY

"Managing is about dealing with a large variety of centres of the world. This is especially difficult when you believe that you are the centre of the world yourself. This book is bringing enlightenment into the business world. It has helped many of us let go of our self-centric attitude."

Franck Bourdeau, Vision and Strategic Advisor.
FOUNDER OF Z-LEADERSHIP

SUCCEED AS AN

INCLUSIVE

LEADER

Leadership is practised not so much
in words as in attitude and in
actions

LIA NOVEMBER 2018

SUCCEED AS AN
INCLUSIVE
LEADER

Winning leadership habits in a diverse world

THAIS COMPOINT

Published by Déclic International
www.declicinternational.com

First Printing: April 2017
Printed by CreateSpace, an Amazon.com company
ISBN-13: 978-1545166154
ISBN-10: 1545166153

For my parents,

ADAUTO (*in memoriam*),

who taught me the love of justice, and

DARCY,

my greatest role model,

&

For my children,

THOMAS, ARTHUR, and **JULIA**,

the most wonderful gifts I got from life.

"Not everyone can become a great artist, but a great artist can come from anywhere."

—Anton Ego in Ratatouille, a Pixar film

CONTENTS

ABOUT THE AUTHOR

THAIS COMPOINT is an internationally acclaimed author, keynote speaker, trainer and consultant specialising in inclusion and diversity in the corporate world. She is the Founder and CEO of Déclic International, a boutique consultancy based in the UK, with a global outlook. She helps companies and business leaders to build inclusive cultures and diverse teams, so that they can better serve their customers and increase engagement, productivity and innovation. Her speciality is delivering high-impact training and thought-provoking lectures. She is also a Huffington Post contributor.

Thais has over eighteen years of international experience. She has led the inclusion and diversity strategies of three Fortune 500 companies: Vinci, Coca-Cola Enterprises, and Cisco. Prior to that, she audited and assessed the diversity and corporate social responsibility strategies of various companies while she worked at Vigeo Eiris, a global provider of social, environmental and governance research.

Thais's achievements have been acknowledged with thirteen awards worldwide. She was recognized in the US as one of the diversity specialists who advanced diversity in the corporate world (2015 Diversity Leader Award), and as the leader of the best European diversity team (2013 European Diversity Awards).

Thais is a true "world citizen": she fluently speaks five languages, lived in six countries, led projects globally and worked in missions in eighteen countries on four continents. She has a Bachelor degree in Law (Federal University of Bahia), a Master degree in International Relations (Paris-Sorbonne University) and a Post-graduate degree in Human Rights (University of Padua).

On a more personal note, Thais grew up in Brazil, lived half of her life in France, is married and has three children. She's passionate about building a more inclusive world, where people feel free to be themselves and valued, no matter how different they are.

ACKNOWLEDGEMENTS

"You have to find what sparks a light in you so that you in your own way can illuminate the world."
—Oprah Winfrey

It's been a splendid adventure to write this book. I'm profoundly grateful to the amazing human beings who helped me along the journey.

Thanks to Edouard-Malo Henry who generously accepted to write the foreword for this book.

Thanks to my "critical friends" who kindly took the time to review my manuscript: Ahmed Belaidi, Alberto Platz, Chantal Goossens, Franck Bourdeau, Géraldine Vallejo, Gus Sekhon, Inès Duval, Johanna Dickinson, Julia Evangelista, Marc Leymonerie, Rohini Anand, Sofia Greve, Sandra Combet, Stéphanie Oueda, Sunil Sehgal, Sylvain Guyoton, Tanguy de Belair, Véronique Vuillod and William Fullford.

Thanks to the "naturally" inclusive leaders who I met throughout my career and who showed me what inclusion looked like in practice: An Vermeulen, Bernard Galtier, Caroline Cater, Geneviève Ferone, Jean-Baptiste Duguet, Jean Monville, John Donovan, KP Singh Baghat, Nigel Miller, Nurit Hattab, Philippe Lamboley and Tunji Akintokun.

Thanks to my dear friend Herley Roger Brito for his invaluable help with the book marketing strategy.

Thanks to my "YouTube" mentors whose motivational messages kept me going: Brendon Burchard, Chris Franklin, Erico Rocha, Flavia Melissa, Marie Forleo, Oprah Winfrey and Paula Abreu.

Thanks to my incredible family members whose support and advice are priceless: Adriana, Aline, Andrea, Angélique, Antonio, Clément, Darcy, Fabiola, Fernanda, François, Guy, Jacques, Jérôme, João, Mariem, Matheus, Pedro, Sofia, Tatiana, Véronique and Vitoria.

Last but not least, thanks to the most amazing husband on earth, Elie, for believing in me.

FOREWORD

I was confronted for the first time to a really diverse environment when I left my native Europe for 6 years to take up a new professional challenge in Australia. Being originally from a remote and traditional part of Western France, it was quite a challenge to adjust, not only to a new language but also to a very different society. Almost half of Australians are not born in Australia, and the population is an impressive melting pot. Being emerged abruptly in this new environment, I realised how energizing (although destabilizing to start with) it is to reassess most of one's own beliefs and to learn how to work with diversified teams.

I later lived a similar experience over a 5-year posting in Canada where the mix of cultures is also fairly impressive and the society open and inclusive. I learned from experience that, in the corporate world, the development and the promotion of diversity is key to a company's creativity, level of energy, and ultimately perennial success. A company that doesn't develop the diversity of its talents is at risk of losing contact with its environment, of misunderstanding with subtlety its clients' needs, and in these times of great uncertainty, of not picking up on the "weak signals." Developing the diversity of our talents is kind of subscribing a Life Insurance, a way of setting out on a long-term performance trend.

Listening to CEO's speeches and reading the abundant literature on the question, this may seem to be stating the obvious. There is hardly a message on HR key priorities or from a CEO on people being the main assets of the firm, not mentioning the attention paid to the diversity of talents. But then facts are stubborn: diversity indicators in most of the companies progress desperately slowly, in particular, those relating to gender diversity. "It's only a matter of time," "It will naturally happen," "The problem is being solved."

When diversity issues arise in a conversation in the workplace, I am often struck by the unrealistic conventional wisdom I hear. As if the battle had been won and was mostly behind us now. As if we could rest on our laurels and things would automatically move in the right direction. I believe this is absolutely not the case, on the contrary. Based on the current trends in most of the working places, it would take another 50 years at least to reach some sort of equal opportunities environment between females and males at every level of companies' management circles.

As always in a professional environment, addressing such a matter implies strong and authentic involvement of the leader, a rigorous project management approach, and a well-structured follow-up process. This is very well addressed by Thais Compoint in her "Inclusive Leadership Propeller Model" which is an innovative, smart and practical way to implement such a policy. Thais is a true expert and professional of diversity and inclusion, being herself at the crossroad of different cultures and having dedicated most of her professional life to this essential matter. She is truly convinced, genuine, and authentic, and her book is a major contribution which will prove to be extremely useful to so many senior executives.

I would also like to stress another dimension to diversity from a personal standpoint: promoting a more diverse environment is also for each of us a human adventure in which we learn a great deal about ourselves. Accepting to discover other people's diversity is taking the opportunity of discovering or rediscovering our own. We all have extremely rich personalities with lots of potentialities, but we have shaped our behaviours under the influence of our own experiences. To adjust or conform to our environment, we have imposed limits on ourselves. It's a pity as our singularity or uniqueness is truly formed by the combination of everything we are. The best way to find out about the richness of our own nature is to be confronted to diversity. The more we accept others, the richer we become. In the same way, as companies must break silos, we must break the walls and the restrictions that prevent us from being truly ourselves. Expressing our singularity through diversity is a fantastic challenge. The most beautiful one I believe, both for the company and for us as individuals.

Edouard-Malo Henry
Group Head of Human Resources
SOCIÉTÉ GÉNÉRALE

INTRODUCTION

"Simplicity is the ultimate sophistication."
—Leonardo Da Vinci

The inclusion and diversity paradox

Many years ago, in 1998 to be precise, I was living in Italy. I had just got married to my French husband, and together we happily moved to Padua, a beautiful little town close to Venice.

Once, I was watching the news, and the journalist announced the results of an intriguing survey. What were Italian children most afraid of? Was it losing their parents? Getting lost? Finding out that they were adopted? No. What they feared the most were the "extracomunitàri," immigrants from outside the European Union. Children in Italy were more afraid of immigrants than they were of the traditional bogeyman! Suddenly I realised I was an "extracomunitaria," since I was born and raised in Brazil.

Coincidently, I was writing an academic paper on the impact of immigration on the Italian economy. Countless studies demonstrated the positive impact of immigrants in the economy. How come such a positive thing, rationally, could be perceived as such a negative thing, emotionally? Since then, I became fascinated with how human beings relate to other human beings who are perceived as different.

For this reason, I became an inclusion and diversity specialist in the corporate world. And in corporations, I've found a similar paradox. Countless studies demonstrate the strong correlation between inclusion and diversity and business performance. For instance, companies with the highest representation of women in senior management deliver 34 percent greater returns to investors.[1] Ethnically diverse companies are 35 percent more likely to outperform financially.[2] Diversity and inclusion is even being used as an investment tool: Thompson Reuters created the first D&I index with the top 100 companies for diversity and inclusion performance. Yet, corporations struggle to achieve diversity, particularly at senior management levels. Although the business case for diversity is clear, workplace culture and the mindset of management top the list of obstacles for a more inclusive workplace.[3]

Actionable insights to make inclusion happen

In my eighteen years of professional experience, I've met many open-minded leaders who believe inclusion and diversity can make them more successful. They want to make it happen. They want to be inclusive leaders, i.e. leaders capable of successfully leading people with different backgrounds. In other words, leaders capable of attracting, inspiring and influencing people of all genders and ages, with different cultures, abilities, and lifestyles. But they don't know exactly what they need to do. They may lack the confidence to deal with prejudices or feel fearful of positively discriminating. That's usually because:

- They lack information;
- They're exposed to impractical information, including superficial training, which raises awareness about the problems without developing the skills to solve them;
- Or they are confused by an overload of fragmented information that disconnects different inclusion and diversity dimensions such as gender, generations, disability, nationality, ethnicity, religion, sexual orientation, work-life balance, etc.

If you've ever struggled with the lack of actionable information on inclusion and diversity, you're not alone. An Oxford Economics survey showed that only 28 percent of global executives think their leaders are prepared to lead a diverse workforce.[4] Other research showed that 49 percent of managers don't know what to do to improve gender diversity, the most high-profile of all diversity topics.[5] I can safely assume that managers don't feel better equipped when it comes to other diversity topics.

This book is inspired by the open-minded leaders I've met, and it's my gift to them. It brings together the most relevant and practical knowledge on how to become an inclusive leader and boost your team's performance as a result. It's a simple, effective and action-oriented toolkit.

Are you ready to succeed as an inclusive leader?

You're in the right place if you're an open-minded business leader or manager looking for new ways to increase engagement, productivity, and creativity in your team. You're in the right place if you're a human resources professional or an inclusion and diversity practitioner looking for concrete tips to create an inclusive culture. You're also in the right place if you're a curious human being, looking for a refreshing perspective on inclusion and diversity, and wishing to contribute to a more inclusive world, where people feel free to be themselves and valued, no matter how different they are.

You're NOT in the right place if you're interested in the compliance aspects and legal requirements related to inclusion and diversity. You're NOT in the right place neither if you want a complete guide to promote inclusion and diversity in organisations. Inclusive leadership is the most crucial aspect of any inclusion and diversity strategy, but it's not the only one. You need to take a systemic approach and review systems, processes, policies, and communications to transform an entire organisation. We're focusing here on the leadership behaviours that create an inclusive culture.

Baby steps to create exponential change anywhere

Many years ago, when I was working at a social and environmental rating agency, I made a study to identify the most inclusive and diverse companies among the top 600 public-listed companies in Europe. The key insight from that study was that a company performance on diversity was more linked to the leadership willingness to make progress than to the company's industry or geography. You could find excellent companies in industries and countries that, on average, were not doing very well. The contrary was also true: some companies were poor performers—in industries and geographies that scored relatively high for diversity. Since then I became convinced that no matter where you are, you can create an inclusive culture, especially at the team level. And I've seen this happening in several organisations throughout my career. This book focuses on your influence zone as a leader, and more specifically, on the habits that you can develop, day in day out, to create an inclusive and diverse team. It's all about the baby steps that you can take to create exponential change over time, wherever you are, without having to change or create policies and procedures.

What you'll learn

Part I is about the basics to get started. You'll discover:

- What inclusive leadership is and why it helps you to succeed.
- The inclusion and exclusion mechanisms, such as unconscious biases, that are common across all types of human differences.
- The inclusive mindset, skills, and habits you need to develop in different leadership situations.
- How to assess and improve your inclusive leadership skills.

Part II delves into the specific barriers and inclusive leadership habits related to different inclusion and diversity dimensions: gender, generations, disability, nationality, ethnicity, religion, sexual orientation, and work-life integration. You can move around and select the different chapters according to your own interests and needs.

A shortcut to eighteen years of experience of a leading expert

"Succeed as an inclusive leader" is a shortcut to eighteen years of operational experience of an internationally acclaimed inclusion and diversity specialist who has led the inclusion and diversity strategies of three Fortune 500 companies in a row, and interviewed over 2000 leaders and employees in eighteen countries:

- It's packed with real-life examples and concrete tips.
- It's based on what works in practice and on what matters most.
- It's grounded on the latest business studies and academic research.

Becoming the leader everyone wants to work with

After reading this book, you'll be confident to embrace differences and equipped to:

- Identify talent when it comes in different sizes and shapes.
- Attract, inspire, and influence people of all genders and ages and with different cultures, abilities, and lifestyles.
- Increase engagement, productivity, and innovation in your team.

You might become the leader everyone wants to work with (if you're not already), because you'll have an enhanced ability to achieve your goals while bringing out the best in the people around you. You'll also be able to show evidence of your inclusion and diversity knowledge to the increasing number of organisations that consider inclusive leadership skills when recruiting and promoting.

All of it with a bonus: you'll become more successful while building a better world. A world where anyone can succeed, no matter how different they are.

Why would you say no to such a great opportunity, literally at your fingertips?

PART I

GETTING THE BASICS RIGHT

"You can practice shooting eight hours a day, but if your technique is wrong, then all you become is very good at shooting the wrong way."
—Michael Jordan

The very first step to succeed as an inclusive leader is to have a solid understanding of:

- **What** inclusion and diversity mean
- **Why** inclusion and diversity matter
- **How** exclusion and inclusion happen
- **Where** you stand regarding your own inclusive leadership skills

PART I is a must-read since it lays the fertile ground for your inclusive leadership habits to germinate and flourish over time.

1

WHAT ARE WE TALKING ABOUT?

"The greatest distance between two people is
misunderstanding."
—Anonymous

**Why you should always ask people what they mean by inclusion
and diversity**

If you ask people around you to tell you what they put behind the words
inclusion, diversity, and inclusive leadership, you'll be amazed by the
variety of answers. How people define these terms is influenced by their
personal experiences, the countries where they live, and the
organisations they work at.

I once started working for a global company and decided to meet all
senior leaders to understand their expectations. As I started my round of
interviews, I realised that although everybody was talking about
"diversity," most of them meant gender diversity. In Brazil, diversity in
companies is mostly associated with disability, because of legal
requirements to employ disabled people. I once attended a glamorous
European diversity event, and as the organisers were LGBT (lesbian, gay,
bisexual and transsexual) activists, most conversations related to LGBT
inclusion.

Inclusion is an even more challenging concept. The word simply
doesn't exist in many languages. I couldn't get the word translated into
Swedish. In France, it's often translated as "integration," which can
actually mean the opposite of inclusion. And inclusive leadership is an
emerging concept. Different authors propose different definitions.

Three pragmatic definitions that you can adopt or adapt

The definitions I'm proposing are simple and pragmatic, reflect the latest developments in the inclusion and diverse field, and work across countries. Feel free to adopt or adapt them.

- **Diversity is the mix** of visible and invisible differences such as differences in gender, age, disability, nationality, ethnicity, religion, sexual orientation, communication, thinking and working styles, education, professional experience, social background, etc. Diversity is endless and is like an iceberg: there are aspects that are very visible (such as gender, age, skin colour) and others that are under the water line (such as education and thinking style). Ultimately, we're looking for the diversity of thoughts and perspectives that come with all different life experiences and backgrounds. That's what some call cognitive diversity.

Based on the above definition, there's already a lot of diversity within an individual; nobody fits just one box and some aspects of diversity change over time (age, for instance). We all bring some type of difference to the workplace. The question is, how free are we to express those differences? Often the diversity that's already in organizations is underutilised. That's why inclusion is crucial.

- **Inclusion is the culture** that makes you feel valued and free to be yourself, even if you look, think and behave differently from the majority. It's culture where people feel their different opinions, behaviors, and needs are taken into account. An inclusive culture gives you a sense of belonging that prevents you from feeling like an outsider.

Once I heard a white male business leader sharing with the audience why he was a big supporter of inclusion and diversity initiatives. He said that his main difference was not visible from the outside. Although he had no accent, he was born and raised in a communist country. He felt really different in this respect from most of his US colleagues. His company inclusion and diversity strategy had made him feel comfortable revealing this part of his self and made him a happier person at work.

Increasingly, specialists underline the importance of inclusion over diversity. Personally, I prefer to say "inclusion and diversity," rather than "diversity and inclusion," in order to emphasize such importance. That's because to attract, develop and retain diverse talents, you need an inclusive culture. You also need an inclusive culture to reap the benefits of a diverse team: if people don't feel included, they're unlikely to bring their full selves to work and give their best. If people can't share their different perspectives because they don't feel safe, it's not possible to improve decision making and to innovate. Finally, diversity without inclusion can lead to an increase in conflicts that can be counterproductive.

- **Inclusive leadership is the ability to lead successfully diverse people**. Inclusive leaders know how to attract, inspire and influence people with different backgrounds. People of all genders and ages, with different cultures, abilities, and lifestyles. That's why they excel at getting the most out of their teams. They play a key role in building diverse teams and creating an inclusive culture.

It's like having the perfect meal: you need a chef (the inclusive leader) who knows how to choose the good ingredients (diversity) and how to combine them using the perfect recipe (inclusion).

Four misconceptions you should get rid of:

- *Diversity is NOT about positive discrimination*

  This is the single biggest objection and misunderstanding about diversity. That's the question I get asked over and over as soon as I tell people what I do. "Oh, diversity; is this the thing about positive discrimination and quotas?" The point is not to hire or promote a person only because she or he belongs to a minority group, forgetting all about talent. The point is to remove the barriers, often unconscious, that prevent us from recognising talent when it comes in different sizes and shapes, in the first place.

We tend to fish in the same talent pools, and look for a certain type of people, often those who look like ourselves. Legal quotas (mandatory and set by governments) about women on boards, or disabled people, for instance, and corporate diversity targets (what companies intend to achieve as a result of their actions) force us to fish in other talent pools in order to reach out for and to consider qualified people who we tend to overlook.

Diversity is about widening our talent pools, not narrowing them. By fishing in bigger pools, you increase your chances of finding the right talent.

In all cases, decisions should always focus on skills and competence. When you hire, promote or dismiss people. Poor performers should not be tolerated just because they are "diverse." Never fall into the trap of believing that you must choose between diversity and quality.

- ***Inclusion is NOT about accommodating minorities***

  Inclusion is about adapting to everybody's differences, including those differences that the "majority" brings. If you focus only on minorities, you alienate the majority that deserves to feel included as much as anyone else. This is one of the reasons why so many people reject inclusion and diversity initiatives: because they don't feel part of it.

- ***Inclusive leadership is NOT only about recruiting***

  So many times, managers tell me, "We are not hiring at the moment; there's nothing we can do about diversity right now." I also hear human resources business partners tell me, "You should talk to our talent acquisition team; hiring is not my responsibility," as an answer to my question about how they embed inclusion and diversity into what they do. Inclusive leadership applies to all management situations. It influences how you communicate, hire, onboard, promote, develop, reward, and dismiss people. It's also about the working conditions you provide, and most importantly, the work culture you create.

2

WHY BOTHER ABOUT INCLUSIVE LEADERSHIP?

"Twenty percent of any change is knowing how, but eighty percent is knowing why."
—Tony Robbins

Why should you care about inclusive leadership?

Why would you spend your precious time developing inclusive leadership skills? The skills to lead successfully diverse teams? After all, most probably you've lived most of your life without them, and maybe you're doing just fine.

I've met leaders who have a clear vision of how inclusion and diversity contribute to their businesses and their careers and are good at articulating their vision to others. But such leaders are rare. I've also met leaders whose values were so strong that they didn't care about the business case for inclusion and diversity. They were even against it. They'd say to me, "This is the right thing to do. Why do I need a business case to treat people properly?" But such leaders had a harder time influencing others to create an inclusive culture.

For some authors, the business case for diversity is so obvious, that business leaders asking for it are either aliens or don't care.[6] I think it's important to review and customise your inclusion and diversity business case. As an inclusive leader, you should not only have clarity on it; you should also be good at sharing your vision with others. Here are the key reasons why becoming an inclusive leader gives you a competitive advantage.

Six key global trends that inclusive leaders navigate more easily

There are major demographic and cultural trends affecting the workplace and the marketplace globally. Inclusive leaders can navigate such changes more easily. Given their connections with diverse talents, they have a more 360° view of the world. They are better equipped to anticipate and understand the evolving needs of increasingly diverse customers and workers.

- **Women play an increasingly important role in the economy**. Women are sixty percent of graduates in industrialised countries and influence up to eighty percent of purchasing decisions.[7]

- **Societies are more multi-cultural.** Cross-border migration has grown 42 percent in the last decade, from 150 million to 214 million migrants, with most traffic directed toward OECD countries.[8] One in ten Europeans lives outside their country of birth.[9] In the US, ethnic minorities will be nearly 60 percent of the population by 2060.[10]

- **The workplace is more multigenerational.** With longer life spans and the rise or abolishment of the retirement age in many countries, we'll tend to extend our work lives. Thus, four to five generations working together will become increasingly commonplace.

- **Societies are more accepting of same-sex relationships**. Same-sex marriage is becoming more common in Western countries, and it's now legal in fifteen countries.

- **The proportion of people with disabilities is increasing**. Currently, fifteen percent of the global population has some form of disability. This number is increasing due to the aging of the population, improved medical treatments helping manage long-term health problems, and the reclassification of what we consider to be a disability.[11]

- **The war for talent will become stronger**. Despite projected growth in the global population, due to the ageing population, the working age population is expected to decline in many countries.[12] In the European labour market, 2010 marked the first time more workers retired than joined the workforce. The labour gap (gap between the demand and the offer of skilled workers) will surge to forty million by 2030.[13]

Seven demonstrated benefits of inclusion and diversity

A Belgian senior leader once told me how the group dynamics had changed for better since more women had joined his executive leadership team. The discussions had become more respectful, and out of the box ideas became more frequent. I've heard several similar accounts. Usually, for diversity to bring results, you need to reach a critical mass of thirty percent of diverse individuals in a team. If you have less than that, individuals who are different from the majority will tend to mimic the behaviours of the majority group and the change in team dynamics will not be as visible.

Beyond people's positive experiences, several studies show that inclusion and diversity bring benefits in at least seven areas. Here's a sample of such studies:

- **Financial performance**
  - ✓ Ethnically diverse companies are 35 percent more likely to outperform financially.[14]
  - ✓ Companies with the highest representation of women in senior management deliver 34 percent greater returns to investors.[15]
- **Customer service**
  - ✓ Employees of firms with diverse teams are 70 percent likelier to report that the firm captured a new market in the previous year.[16]
  - ✓ 71 percent of LGBT (Lesbians, gays, bisexuals and transsexuals) and 82 percent of allies are more likely to purchase from a company that supports LGBT equality.[17]

- **Talent attraction**
  - ✓ Two-thirds of respondents in a Glassdoor survey say a diverse workforce is important when choosing where to work.[18]
- **Productivity**
  - ✓ The "Aristotle project" was a research done by Google to find out the secret of productive teams. They discovered that the key characteristic of productive teams is the feeling of psychological safety generated by a culture where people feel heard and safe to be themselves.[19] In other words, an inclusive culture.
- **Engagement**
  - ✓ 96 percent of global executives believe having an inclusive and diverse workforce improves employee engagement.[20]
- **Innovation**
  - ✓ Teams made up of even proportions of men and women come up with the most innovative ideas.[21]
- **Decision making**
  - ✓ A diverse group of problem solvers will outperform consistently a group of best problem solvers.[22] That's because diversity increases the collective ability to see the problems from different angles.

There's an interesting parallel made between diverse talents, ecosystems and financial systems. Just like biodiversity increases productivity and resilience, and diverse investment portfolios mitigate risks, diverse and inclusive teams mitigate groupthink and correlate with higher financial performance.[23]

How lack of inclusion can cost you money

If you have team members feeling excluded or unfairly treated, it won't take long for them to become disengaged, to take sick leave and eventually leave your team or organisation.

- **Lack of engagement**
  - ✓ Lack of engagement costs on average 35 percent of companies' payrolls in the US.[24]
- **Absenteeism**
  - ✓ One percent of absenteeism is equivalent to one percent of the payroll.[25]
- **Turnover**
  - ✓ The cost to replace an employee can go from sixteen percent of annual salary for low paid jobs up to 213 percent of annual salary for highly paid executive positions.[26]

Moreover, unhappy employees can sue you, and talk about their negative experiences on the internet and social media, which can severely damage your reputation and your organisation's as well.

Don't let the fear of resistance paralyse you

In a nutshell, inclusion and diversity help you navigate demographic changes, attract talent, serve customers, increase performance, engagement, productivity, innovation and the quality of decision making. They also help you save costs related to attrition, absenteeism, lack of engagement, lawsuits and negative publicity. Promoting inclusion and diversity is also the right thing to do from a moral perspective.

Despite all of this, I always find managers who need more convincing to get started in the inclusive leadership journey. I was having a conversation with a friend, who happens to be a senior business leader, and for him, a key roadblock is the fact that problems are complex and that any attempt to change things in this area will be confronted with resistance. He's right, in the sense that any change encounters resistance, and you must deal with it. But I hope you don't let the fear of resistance paralyse you. Because the best antidote to fear is action. In this case, the action is to get started and to keep going with the small baby-steps that you'll learn in the upcoming chapters.

What is your unique business case for leading inclusively?

I hope that by now you're convinced that becoming an inclusive leader is a good idea. If you are not convinced, maybe you picked the wrong book, sorry about that. This book's main topic is "how" to become an inclusive leader, not "why." If you are convinced and want your inclusive leadership journey to be sustainable, you need to identify exactly how becoming an inclusive leader might help you solve your current problems or create opportunities for you. You need to find out which pain points your inclusive leadership skills will help address. The following exercise helps you identify these areas.

EXERCISE

Select the three questions that most resonate with you.

1. Do you need to innovate in products, services or processes?
2. Do you need to better understand customer's needs or expand your customer base?
3. Do you need to avoid group-thinking?
4. Do you need to attract more talents?
5. Do you need to increase retention?
6. Do you need to reduce absenteeism?
7. Do you need to increase engagement?
8. Do you need to increase productivity?
9. Do you need to keep people on board as they grow old?
10. Do you need to improve the knowledge transfer within your team?
11. Do you need to improve communications within your team?
12. Do you need to improve the working atmosphere?
13. Do you need to feel more aligned with your personal values or want to make a positive impact in the world?
14. Do you need to improve your business image and reputation?
15. Do you need to show your hierarchy you care about inclusion and diversity?

The questions above are the main areas that can be impacted positively by inclusive leadership. The three questions you've just identified represent your most compelling reasons for improving your inclusive leadership skills. We'll call them your inclusive leadership drivers. Write them down because you'll need them to build your personalised action plan in a way that serves you best.

My inclusive leadership drivers

#1

(Example: avoid group-thinking)

#2

(Example: increase engagement)

#3

(Example: reduce absenteeism)

The power and the beauty of it

No matter why you want to be an inclusive leader in the first place, for value-driven reasons or business-driven reasons, you'll be glad to find out that the side effects will be positive.

If you are interested in inclusive leadership because of your own values or personal situation, the business impact of your actions will be positive. This is a question I love asking the amazing inclusive leaders I meet: "What motivates you?" Very often the reasons are very personal. I met a French manufacturing site director who excelled at accommodating disabled workers. He told me that in his family, he had two people with severe disabilities, and that was why he became very keen on disability inclusion. I met an American CEO who was a great diversity champion. When I asked him why, he told me that growing up in Mississippi in the 60s, he had seen so many racial atrocities that he became very sensitive to justice. He had also seen the very few female engineer students in his college achieving the best grades, and he became convinced of the value of gender balance. There's even research that shows that the most supportive male leaders when it comes to gender diversity have daughters!

However, if you're becoming an inclusive leader for purely business-driven reasons, you're also helping to create a better world.

That's the power and the beauty of inclusion and diversity.

3

HOW EXCLUSION HAPPENS

"Thinking is difficult. That's why most people judge."
—Carl Jung

Inclusion and diversity don't come naturally

If inclusion and diversity are so good for business as so many studies demonstrate, why is it then that they don't come naturally? That's a very common question. It's exactly the question I was asked by a Bulgarian gentleman I met during a garden party in London, days after the UK Brexit vote.

Indeed, there's robust evidence of lack of diversity in corporations, particularly at senior levels. And there's also evidence that discrimination is widespread:

- Women are only 22 percent of senior managers in the G7 countries[27] and earn on average 15 percent less than men in similar positions.[28]

- In the US, CVs with white-sounding names receive fifty percent more callbacks for interviews than identical CVs with black-sounding names.[29] Research shows similar results for CVs with foreign-sounding names in European countries.

- Age discrimination is the most widely experienced form of discrimination across Europe.[30]

- In Europe, twenty percent of LGBT (Lesbian, gay, bisexual and transsexual) people and twenty percent of people with disabilities feel unfairly treated because of their sexual orientation or disability.[31] [32]

- In France, 29 percent of private sector employees say they have already felt discriminated against.[33]

The illusion of objectivity

If you ask people around you: "Do you think women are less capable than men?" or 'Do you think black people are less smart than white people?" people will be shocked. Most of us genuinely believe that talent doesn't have sex, age, or skin colour.

Based on the "talent comes in all shapes" assumption, if we are focusing on skills and competencies when hiring and promoting, we should "naturally" end up with diverse organisations. It seems logical. But this is not happening. Not only because of social, historical, and economic reasons. We often fail to see talent when it comes in sizes and shapes we're not used to.

Most of us believe we hire and promote people based on merit. A French managing director in the insurance industry once told me, "I don't even see people's sex, skin colour or age; I treat everybody the same, I don't have prejudices, naturally." We wrongly believe that we don't have prejudices. This might be our intention at a conscious level, but our unconscious that dictates our behaviour 95% of the time is always judging people on the way they look.[34] This gap between what we say and what we do is called cognitive dissonance. Research tells us that it takes a tenth of a second to form an impression of a stranger.[35] The fact is, we're terrible at evaluating people objectively. We're deluded by what Yale psychologist David Armor calls the illusion of objectivity, the notion that we're free from the bias we're so quick to recognise in others.[36] In fact, the more objective we think we are, the more biased we are. Research showed the "paradox of meritocracy": the ironic finding that people and organizations that assert they are meritocracies are typically less meritocratic in practice than their peers.[37]

How our brain works

Scientists estimate that we're exposed to as many as eleven million pieces of information at any one time, but our brain can only functionally deal with 40.[38] There's an overload of information for a reduced cognitive capacity. To cope with it, our brain developed two parts: an unconscious part and a conscious part. The Psychologist and Nobel Prize winner Daniel Kahneman called them System 1 and System 2. System 1 is unconscious, automatic, fast and effortless. System 2 is conscious, deliberate, slow and effortful.[39]

Our unconscious brain is very useful. It creates categories that simplify information and help us navigate the world safely. It's responsible for our survival instinct, as it allows us to quickly and effortlessly detect danger and trigger the fight, fly or freeze reaction. This mechanism has been very helpful during the cave times. And it's still helpful in everyday situations, like when you see a big dog running towards you. Our unconscious mind also helps us to do things without having to think about it, like brushing our teeth, taking a shower and driving to work. This is handy because thinking consciously consumes a lot of energy. Our brain uses more energy than any other human organ, accounting for up to twenty percent of the body's energy consumption, although it weighs less than two percent of the body mass.[40]

Regarding human relations, our unconscious brain categorises people using easily observed criteria such as gender, age, skin colour and weight. That's how we create stereotypes, which are beliefs about a category of people. Biases are judgements about people based on a stereotype. I'll give you a simple example about people who wear glasses (category). I might hold the stereotype that says *People who wear glasses are smart.* My son introduces me to his new friend, who wears glasses, and I think to myself, *She'll be a good influence on him*, because I assume she's smart. I'm judging her without knowing her (bias). I've done all this without realising it. My unconscious mind was in charge.

The problem is, if you only rely on your unconscious mind, you're prone to making mistakes and behaving inappropriately. For example, not long after the Paris terrorist attack on January 2015, a human resources director reported to me how ashamed he was of his behaviour during a flight. He saw a man dressed in a traditional Arab outfit sitting in front of him. He assumed that the passenger was Muslim (category). He thought the Muslim passenger was a terrorist (bias) based on the belief that *Muslims are terrorists* (stereotype). He then changed seats. That's why our conscious mind needs to step in at times, especially when we're taking decisions about people.

Four things you need to know about stereotypes:

- **They are misleading**

  Stereotypes maybe statistically wrong. For instance, often when people hear the word disability, they think of people on wheelchairs, yet, wheelchairs users make up only two to three percent of all disabled people. Even when stereotypes are true most of the time, they will never be true all the time. Individuals are unique. I'm Brazilian, and I don't like football, yet most Brazilians love football.

- **They are difficult to get rid of**

  Stereotypes provide a sense of order and predictability that reassures us. That's why once you have stereotypes about a certain category, you'll filter information to confirm them and disregard information that contradicts them. For instance, you believe the British are gentlemanlike; if you come across a rude British, you'll tell yourself, *This is not the typical British person,* and your stereotype will remain intact. Even when you see a group of British hooligan on TV destroying a stadium.

- **They influence our self-image**

  Stereotypes don't only influence the way you see others. You also internalise stereotypes about the categories you belong to, from a very early age. The historical "doll test" conducted by Dr. Kenneth Clark with black children is a good illustration of this. In his experiment, he asked black children to choose a doll to play with, and most of them chose a white doll, because they saw it as the "nice" doll, whereas the black doll was seen as "mean." A 2017 study revealed that 6-year-old girls are less likely than boys to believe that members of their gender are "really, really smart." The same study showed that in 2014, American parents Googled "Is my son a genius?" more than twice as often as they Googled "Is my daughter a genius?"[41] A Harvard's global online research study, which included over 200,000 participants, showed that 76 percent of people, both men and women, are gender biased. They tend to think of men as better suited for careers and of women as better suited as homemakers.[42] A female finance director told me how disappointed she was when her daughter announced that she wanted to get into the Army. The same director realised that if her son had told her the same thing, her reaction would have been very different.

- **Stereotypes versus generalizations**

A generalization is an insight based on empirical evidence about a group of people. It's a real distinctive behaviour in a group of people (not individuals). It's a starting point that can help you understand and adapt to people's behaviours. For instance, *Teenagers tend to reject what their parents say* (generalization). Now that I have three teenagers at home, I can see this happening. Thanks to the generalization, I'm not surprised. I read about it. I even found out that this is a healthy sign. I don't take it personally. A stereotype is an ending point; it's when you apply beliefs about groups to every single group member without questioning. *Karl is German; he must love eating sausages.* You invite Karl for dinner, and you cook sausages. This is stereotyping. *Karl is German. Germans eat lots of sausages.* You invite Karl for dinner and ask him, "I was thinking of cooking sausages, how would you like that?" This is making good use of a generalisation. By the way, Karl is vegan... Some people hate hearing generalisations about groups of people because they haven't grasped this subtle but important distinction between stereotypes and generalisations based on empirical evidence. Making a good use of generalisations is key for inclusive leaders. For instance, lots of studies show that women tend to be less confident than men. This doesn't mean every single woman will be less confident. But this is an important information that will have an impact in the way many women behave, and in the way you'll interpret their behaviours.

From thoughts to action

I'm Brazilian, and I lived in France many years. Stereotypes in France about Brazilians tend to be positive. The French associate Brazilians with samba, music, dance, beach, football, happy people, beautiful girls. Often when I say to the French that I'm Brazilian, I can feel their positive biases towards me. People often smile at me.

But being a Brazilian has not always been an advantage: I once was living in Italy, and I was trying to rent a flat. Landlords would ask me over the phone, "Where do you come from?" Whenever I said that I was Brazilian, suddenly the flat wasn't available anymore. It took me two weeks to realise that being a Brazilian was an issue. A bartender told me that in that city, people associated Brazilian women with prostitutes. Based on a stereotype (a belief that Brazilian women are prostitutes), not only were landlords biased against me, they also discriminated against me. Discrimination is not only a judgement or thought, like a bias. It is an action, punishable by law, the action of treating someone less favourably on the grounds of race, age, sex, or any other protected characteristic (nationality for that matter).

Bias also can influence our behaviours in small but powerful ways, and generate micro-inequities. Micro-inequities are subtle, often unconscious, messages that devalue, discourage and impair performance.[43] Micro-inequities can appear on the way you listen to people, ask questions, greet them and connect with them on a personal level. A group of researchers is even developing an algorithm that can detect hidden racial bias from a person's body language. [44] I've seen a French senior director who would kiss all his female colleagues, except one, which made her feel awful. A known micro-inequity is called "manterrupting," which is the fact that men tend to interrupt women much more than they interrupt men. In fact, women tend to be nearly three times more interrupted than men in meetings.[45] You can see this happening as well on TV shows involving debates. Another phenomenon is called "mansplaining," which means "to explain something to someone, typically a man to woman, in a manner regarded as condescending or patronizing."[46]

Biases affect all areas of our lives: even the way we react to hurricanes! Research has found that there's a dramatic difference between the average death rates of the storms named for men (23) and those named for women (45). Unconsciously, people assume female named hurricanes to be gentler and less violent, and as a result, prepare less for it.[47] You wouldn't think that bias impact the way we appreciate music, would you? Yet, when symphony orchestras started using blind auditions by placing candidates behind screens and drapes, the number of women in the five leading orchestras in the US increased fivefold.[48] The blind auditions didn't work in the beginning because, as women were wearing heels, the members of the jury could hear a click for female musicians that they couldn't for male musicians. The blind auditions really started working once female musicians were asked to avoid heels. In that way the members of the jury could not know the gender identity of the musiciens.

Who? Me, biased?

Bias reminds me of jealousy. We don't like to admit we're jealous. At times we're not even aware of our jealousy, but people can see how our behaviours are driven by jealousy. Similarly, most people are not aware of their biases, and even when they are, they won't admit it. Yet, we're all biased to some extent. And becoming aware of it is the first step to mitigating the impact of biases. Experiments show that people strengthen their prejudices when they are forced to pretend they don't exist. So, it's important to be able to talk openly about prejudices. But knowing we're all biased is not an excuse to sit down and do nothing about it. The simple awareness without action can actually legitimise and reinforce your biases as well. The message has to be very clear: we're all biased, and we all need to find ways to reduce the impact of biases. It's our responsibility to mitigate the impact of unconscious bias. That's why many corporations, such as Google, Coca-Cola, and Facebook, started training their entire workforce on unconscious bias. Good unconscious bias training not only raises awareness, but it also builds the skills to change behaviours and strengthens objectivity in decision making. Identifying and reducing organisational and individual biases is slowly becoming the norm. According to Future Work Institute, fifty percent of employers in the US will be offering training on unconscious bias by 2019.[49]

Research shows that you can mitigate the impact of bias if you're able to reflect on your decision making as opposed to acting on your first impulse. There are also other useful techniques that can help you. I highly recommend you take the Implicit Association Test that was developed by Harvard University.[50] This scientifically validated test is available online for free, and it allows you to measure your unconscious biases regarding different categories of people. The results can be surprising and might make you feel uncomfortable, but they can make you aware of what you unconsciously associate with different categories of people. You'll learn about other techniques to outsmart biases in the next chapter.

The #1 cause for exclusion

Most people say they appreciate diversity. However, as we've just seen, human beings innately perceive anyone different as a threat because our brain has an evolutionary requirement to do so. Our human tendency is to divide the social world into groups, ingroups (the groups we belong to), and outgroups. As a result, we instinctively treat ingroup members with care and outgroup members with caution. We tend to stay in our comfort zones and connect with and favour people who are just like ourselves. This is called "affinity bias," and is the number one cause for exclusion. Not the fact that we intentionally exclude people who are different from us, even if this can be true in many cases. Unfortunately, some people are deliberately racists, sexists, homophobes, etc. Affinity bias turns meritocracy into a "mirrorocracy" in most organisations.[51] An insidious way affinity bias manifests itself is through the *fit question*. When people ask, "Will he or she fit into our culture?" what they're really looking for is reassurance that the new person is similar to the group. A much better question to ask instead is, "What does he or she add to the group?"

Three other biases closely related to affinity bias

- ### The confirmation bias

  When you like someone, usually because the person is similar to you in some ways, you'll scan the reality in a very selective mode. Everything that confirms your gut feeling will be kept; everything that goes against it will be ignored. And that's how you rationalise opinions that are not based on facts, to begin with, but come from feelings of comfort.

- ### The "halo and horns" effect

  If you like someone, or if you have a high opinion of someone, whatever the person does will be interpreted positively (the halo effect). If you dislike someone, whatever the person does will be interpreted negatively (the horns effect). There's a study where students were asked to interpret the behaviours of rats in a labyrinth. Half of the students were told that the rats had been genetically modified to be very smart. The other half was told that the rats had been genetically modified to be very dumb. As a result, the exact same behaviours were interpreted in completely different ways. For instance, the rats' pause before taking an exit was seen as a sign of intelligence by one group, and as a sign of stupidity by the other group.

- **The pygmalion effect**

  People's behaviours are influenced by our expectations about them. When you like someone or have a high opinion of someone, you implicitly expect the best from that person. That positive expectation acts like an encouragement to do your best. The contrary is also true. When you don't expect much from someone, your negative expectation has a negative consequence on people's performance. A known experiment illustrates well the pygmalion effect. In a school class, teachers were told some students had a high IQ, even though in reality they had average IQs. A few months later, the students who the teachers believed had high IQs had progressed much faster than the other students. Because teachers treated them like smart kids, they started performing like smart kids. This is a big lesson for all of us, not only in the corporate world but also in our private lives, regarding the way we treat our kids…

Pause for a moment and ask yourself: who do you spend the most time with at work? Who do you go for advice? Whose opinion do you ask for in meetings? Do people you hire look like each other? How similar are they to you? I once met a director in the oil and gas industry who told me that the first criteria he looked for on a CV was whether the candidate was a scout. Because he too had been one! No wonder the same director complained about how difficult it was to find qualified candidates. His talent pool was indeed very small: qualified engineers with a scout history.

I could see affinity bias in myself when I was facilitating training sessions in France in a construction company that employed a high number of first and second generation of Portuguese immigrants. When participants had Portuguese sounding names, I realised I had a tendency to look more often to them. Something that I quickly corrected once I became aware of it.

The #2 cause for exclusion

The number two cause for exclusion is our inability to put ourselves in somebody else's shoes. In other words, lack of empathy. I'm referring to both emotional empathy, which means feeling somebody else's pain, and cognitive empathy, which is understanding where people come from, what they think, what they want, and what makes them happy.[52] That's a skill that doesn't come naturally to many people. We tend to assume that others are just like ourselves, that they have the same preferences and needs.

It's true that all human beings want to be happy and loved. In this sense, we're all the same. We share the same humanity; we're all going to die. However, beyond that deeper level of sameness, we are different in the way that we see the world. We have different needs, different thinking, communication and learning styles. We are influenced by different cultures, be it national cultures, generational cultures, industry cultures, corporate cultures. Our family values, religious beliefs (or none), and personal experiences also influence us. Societal expectations on us are not the same, depending on who we are. There's a high risk of excluding people unintentionally if you don't consider such differences.

Why treating others as you'd like to be treated is a mistake

Take the need for flexibility, for instance. I've seen a sales director organise his team meetings always at the same time, very early in the morning. The same director once chose to organise his annual kick-off meeting on the first day back to school. He had grown up children, and a stay-at-home wife, and he didn't realise the impact of his choices on working parents, particularly working parents of young children. The person who told me this story had just changed departments because he wasn't happy working for that director.

Sometimes we fail to take into account basic needs. On another occasion, as I was running focus groups in a factory whose female rates were very low, I found out that in the space where workers spent most of their time, there were no ladies' toilets. The few women working there had to walk a long way to use the ladies' toilets in the reception area. They also felt uncomfortable in the uniforms, that weren't designed to fit the female morphology. They didn't feel welcome in that environment, and their attrition rates were five times higher than men's. When I told the plant director my key findings, he couldn't believe that in his ten years in that plant, he had never noticed that there were no ladies' toilets. He was shocked by his own blindness.

Another example, from a construction site this time: a site director decided to have a barbecue during the summer for all employees. The meat served was pork. And many workers didn't eat pork. Except for the salads, they couldn't eat during the barbecue and felt humiliated during an event that was supposed to thank them for their hard work.

I was once in a corporate dinner with American senior leaders. It was the first time I was meeting them. On the table where I was, they talked for a long time about American football. I couldn't understand most of the conversation and felt uncomfortable. At some point, somebody said, "Let's change the subject; not everybody likes American football." I felt so grateful and could finally start to connect with those around me.

There are endless real life examples similar to the above, and they demonstrate how you can exclude people unintentionally by treating others as you'd like to be treated—which shows that inclusive leadership is not only about taking unbiased decisions. If that were the case, robots would make the perfect inclusive leaders. Empathy is a key skill you need to develop as well.

4

THE THREE SIGNATURE SKILLS OF INCLUSIVE LEADERS

"A good system shortens the road to the goal."
—Orison Swett Marden

By now, you know what you can gain by becoming an inclusive leader, and you understand what's on the way: unconscious bias, particularly affinity bias, and your difficulty to put yourself in other people's shoes. How can you then succeed at building an inclusive and diverse team?

Here's a very simple framework that if applied consistently, in different leadership situations, will allow you to check your blind spots and attract, inspire, and influence people from different backgrounds.

I named it the Inclusive Leadership Propeller Model©. I started applying it years ago in a major soft drinks organisation. I'll never forget how grateful leaders were to learn a straightforward tool that they could simply apply. In this organisation, women representation rates and engagement scores regarding inclusion and diversity went consistently up, following the one-day inclusive leadership training leaders got. The training wasn't the unique factor leading to progress. You've got to be systemic and work on processes, systems, and accountability as well as on building skills to drive change. But the training played a key role in shifting that organisational culture.

Imagine a boat. This boat is your team, and the boat propeller is you, the inclusive leader. For a propeller to work properly, it needs at least three blades. Similarly, you need to consistently apply three skills: fairness, empathy, and proactivity. By doing so, you'll take your boat, or your team, very far. You'll navigate human differences smoothly.

The Inclusive Leadership Propeller Model ©

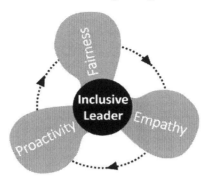

"Fairness is not an attitude. It's a professional skill that must be developed and exercised."
—Brit Hume

#1 Fairness - Are you being fair?

Many people believe that fairness is treating everybody the same. Fairness actually means giving everybody the same opportunities. For this to happen, you have to make sure that your actions don't favour certain categories of people over others. Given the influence of unconscious bias on how you relate to others, you're not naturally fair and objective. You're subjective. This simple awareness in itself already sets you apart from most leaders. Most people genuinely believe they give everybody the same chances, as we saw in the last chapter.

I'm a fan of Star Wars. The one thing that deeply touches me in the saga is this acknowledgement of the "dark side" that exists within each of us and the inner fight of the movie heroes to resist it. There's a great parallel with inclusion: in order to be inclusive, you have to acknowledge "your dark side," the little Darth Vader that exists inside your mind, which is your potential to be biased. Awareness is the greatest antidote to unconscious biases. Just like light is the most powerful thing to get rid of darkness. Your awareness is like a flashlight.

But awareness is not enough. You need to make a conscious effort to mitigate the impact of biases and to put skills and competence at the heart of all decisions you take about people. The underlying belief is that since talent comes in all shapes, by removing the unconscious barriers and truly focusing on skills and competence, you'll increase your chances of building more diverse teams. You also increase your chances of building an inclusive culture, where people feel fairly treated and valued.

To exercise your fairness muscles, you need to practice the following three habits:

- **Identify and challenge biases in yourself and others**
  This includes biases that are explicit—for instance, when you see inappropriate behaviours and remarks—as well as subtle and unconscious biases, which are harder to spot. Never take objectivity for granted. Especially when taking decisions about people. Always ask yourself, *Where's the potential bias in this situation?* Replace the question *Does he/she fit in?* with *What does he/she add to the team?* Write down your first impressions and go beyond them. Take the Implicit Association Tests to find out which biases you have and ask your team to do the same. The more tired, hungry, and under pressure you are, the more prone to bias. Be extra careful under these circumstances.

  A powerful way to challenge biases in yourself and others is to expose yourself and others to counter stereotypical examples and positive role models. I was once in a talent review meeting where a man was being considered "too young" for a promotion. One of the meetings' participants came up with a few examples of people of the same age who had been promoted to similar roles and were doing well. Age then became a non-issue in the discussions.

  A very insidious way bias shows is through jokes and banter. An Algerian man once told me that in his team, whenever something disappeared, his colleagues said that he must have stolen it, as he was the Arab in the team. Everybody laughed, and so did he—because he wanted to feel part of the team. But that made him feel terrible.

It's great to laugh together, but make sure this doesn't happen at the expense of someone.

- **Genuinely follow structured processes instead of simply relying on gut instinct**

  For example, interview candidates using the same questions in the same order; evaluate people's performance simultaneously rather than sequentially; use diverse panels for interviews or ban single-sex panels; during meetings, systematically ask every participant to voice their opinions. Processes that increase accountability and transparence are particularly efficient. For instance, I've seen a company that increased its female rates by requiring all managers hiring or promoting men to explain why they couldn't find a suitable female candidate. Processes don't guarantee unbiased decision making because people tend to rationalise their irrational choices, but they certainly reduce the influence of biases, especially if they are well designed.

- **Look at metrics and history to identify potential biases and track progress**

  When you look at the numbers and in the past, you can see patterns that are invisible to you on a daily basis. On one occasion I was auditing an organisation where there was a strong perception amongst employees that older people were not given the same opportunities. I looked at the numbers, and in the past three years, not a single person over fifty had been hired. Looking at the past was a wake-up call for senior leaders in that organisation that realised an age bias they were completely unaware of. In another occasion, I was in the US, assessing the inclusive culture in a company whose managing director wasn't very willing to talk to me. When I showed to him the gender and ethnic representation numbers in his company and how they compared with the labour market, he was speechless because he was completely unaware of such gaps. He then became a great diversity champion. I strongly recommend you pause to think retrospectively and look at your metrics at least once a year or during key moments, such as before hiring, talent reviews, annual performance, and calibration meetings. Basic metrics to look at include representation by gender, age, and ethnicity (or whatever diversity data is available to you) by level, in recruitment, promotion, attrition, performance, and engagement. You should be looking for proportionality. For instance, if women are thirty percent of your team, they should be thirty percent of promotions. Otherwise, you should find out what's happening. You should also be looking for gaps. For example, if the engagement scores of people over fifty are much lower than those of other age groups, you should inquire.

"People don't care how much you know, until they know how much you care."

—Theodore Roosevelt

#2 Empathy - Are you treating others as they'd like to be treated?

Empathy is the ability to put yourself in other people's shoes so that you can understand how they feel, what drives them, and what they need. Empathy is essential to make others feel included, i.e., respected and valued for who they really are. Empathy also reinforces fairness, since to give everybody the same opportunities means, at times, treating people differently, depending on their needs.

When you put yourself in other people's shoes, you realise what you have in common and also what makes you different. By understanding what you have in common with others, you can better connect with them at a personal level, which is the best way to build trust. By understanding what makes you different, you can adapt. The golden rule—*Treat others as you'd like to be treated*—is outdated in a diverse world. The platinum rule now is, *Treat other as they'd like to be treated.*

You'll become more empathetic by practicing these three key habits:

- **Be curious about people**

  Observe, listen, and ask questions without being intrusive. That's how you connect with people and understand what makes them tick. Inclusive leadership requires constant conversations, from human being to human being, beyond roles. When you share about yourself, you instigate others to do the same. I was once working as a consultant for a leading European group. I had just come back from my third maternity leave and was about to embark on a major training mission that involved a lot of travelling. I went to an event at the group's headquarters, and there I met for the second time the group's CEO, a man at the top of an organisation with over 40,000 employees. He remembered me, my name, and the fact that I had just come back from maternity leave. He asked me how I was and how my baby was. He also asked me if I had the support I needed at home while I was away on the mission. In three minutes, I became his biggest fan. He asked me questions that really mattered to me at that moment. He showed that he cared about me. Questions that my line manager at the time never asked me. My commitment to that mission went up by a thousand times.

- **Be aware of your impact on others**

  To be aware of your impact on others, you should first be aware of your own style and preferences. And then you should ask for feedback. I've known a manager who led a virtual global team. Some team members needed regular feedback about how they were doing but never got it. When I raised the topic with the manager, he told me that he personally didn't need feedback to get going. He associated feedback with bad news. So, he assumed that his team was happy by not hearing from him: *No news = Good news*. The moment he asked for feedback about the way he was providing (or rather not providing) feedback to his team, he realised the negative impact he was having on the team's engagement and performance.

- **Adapt to people's different styles and needs**

  Once you are aware of others' and your preferences and needs, it's important to be able to adapt not only your style but also the work organisation. I've seen a senior human resources leader who was an excellent communicator. She was American and often spoke to non-native English speakers. She carefully chose the words and the pace of her speech to make herself easily understood by her audience. All her videos were subtitled as well, which made life easier also for non-native English speakers. I also once met a site director who decided to open his canteen a bit later during the day to adapt to workers practicing the Ramadan.

"Sometimes if you want to see a change for the better, you have to take things into your own hands."

—Clint Eastwood

#3 Proactivity - Are you accelerating positive change?

Are you ready to wait until 2186 for the world to achieve gender equality? That's the date by when, according to The World Economic Forum, we will achieve gender parity if we continue to progress at the same pace.[53] I have no reason to believe the predictions would be any better for other diversity dimensions.

That's why an inclusive leader ought to be proactive and take initiatives to accelerate change. This doesn't mean doing "positive discrimination" or "reverse discrimination." Positive discrimination happens when you decide that for a given position, you'll hire or promote someone from a minority group, regardless of skills and competence. This is a big mistake. You should never sacrifice your standards. Hiring or promoting someone only because she or he belongs to a minority group is unfair and counterproductive, with negative consequences for everybody involved. That said, it's possible, in many countries, to favour a candidate who will add more diversity to a group, if he or she qualifies for the job as much as other candidates.

This is an example of "positive action." Positive action is key to counteract the ubiquitous influence of unconscious bias. It's key not "because of past wrongs done to one group or another, but because of the everyday wrongs that we can now document are inherent in the ordinary everyday behaviour of good, well-intentioned people."[54]

Being proactive also means taking risks without lowering your standards. When you're looking for candidates with different backgrounds, you might not find people with exactly the same career path as the candidates you're used to. Maybe you'll find people in other industries, or with other degrees. Very often foreign candidates are overlooked because hiring managers are not familiar with their degrees or credentials. Have clarity on what are the essential skills to do a job and those that can be learned once in the role. Some IT companies are successfully increasing their proportion of women by hiring women from other industries and providing them with training on the IT specific skills.

Being proactive is about igniting change. It's like lighting a fire. To make a fire, a good and long-lasting one, you need tinder, until the fire is stable. Similarly, to change the status quo regarding inclusion and diversity, you need some actions that, hopefully, won't be necessary over time, but that are very important to overcome initial barriers until the inclusive culture is part of a team's or organisation's DNA. The better the weather conditions, the less you'll need tinder. But you might need a lot of tinder to set the fire if the weather conditions are not favourable. For instance, if you're working in an environment that's not very open to inclusion and diversity.

Here are the three key habits to flex your proactivity muscles:

- **Raise awareness about inclusion and diversity**
  Raise awareness about inclusion and diversity, and also about your commitment to it. Don't assume candidates, team members, or recruitment agencies know how open you are to inclusion and diversity; tell them. People who are different from the majority are particularly sensitive to this type of message. I once advised a factory

director to make inclusion and diversity part of the conversations with temporary workers' agencies. Six months after, the proportion of ethnic minorities within the temporary works population had gone up by thirty percent. One of the agencies told him that prior to that conversation, they thought the factory director was not very open to diverse candidates... I met a Finance VP who always included diversity as a topic of his annual leadership team meetings. I've known an IT Director in the UK who printed dozens of pins to celebrate the Black History month. He wore it knowing that this would trigger people's curiosity. As they asked questions, he could start the conversation with people and offer them the pins. Use different opportunities to raise the awareness of your team members about different diversity topics. For instance, you can bring somebody to talk to your team during the International women's day, the European disability week, or the international day against homophobia. You can also participate and encourage your team members to participate in employee networks activities, or you can help set up one if they don't exist in your organization.

- **Reach out to diverse candidates**

  This means taking initiatives to increase your chances of finding qualified candidates with a diverse background. For instance, you can decide that your shortlist of candidates should be diverse. This is called the "Rooney rule," and it was introduced by the National Football League in the US as a way to increase the proportion of African American coaches. At the time, African Americans were 65 percent of players, but only ten percent of coaches. The proportion of minority coaches doubled by 2012 as a result of such rule.[55] You can also ban "all male" shortlists; you can systematically send out your job posts to organizations specialised in disabled candidates, partner with universities that have more socially diverse students, guarantee job interviews to qualified disabled people, etc. But be careful not to discriminate members of the majority group. For instance, it's not possible to ask for an only women shortlist of candidates. Or to decide beforehand that you will hire a member of an ethnic minority.

- **Mentor and sponsor diverse people**

  Research shows that mentoring and sponsorship are the biggest accelerators in people's careers. Mentoring is said to increase the possibility that staff will stay by on average one-third.[56] Mentoring is guiding someone. Sponsorship is advocating for someone. In other words, mentoring is what happens when you're in the room; sponsorship is what happens when you aren't in the room.[57] Mentoring and sponsorship help diverse people to understand the unwritten rules of the corporate political game, to boost their confidence, to have access to opportunities. Given the power of affinity bias, people who are different from the majority tend to lack in their networks influential decision makers. We tend to informally mentor and sponsor people who look like ourselves. Take a moment to think about the protégés you've had in your life. And those who have helped in your career. How similar were they to you? How about reaching out to people with different backgrounds facing barriers to enter and to progress in the workplace? You can informally mentor and sponsor people inside and outside your organisation. But it's important that your mentoring or sponsorship effort is authentic. You've got to build a trust relationship with your mentee or protégé; otherwise, it won't work. Check if your company has mentoring or sponsorship programs you could join. You can also promote cross-mentoring within your team by pairing together people from different ages, different cultures… Look at mentoring and sponsorship as reciprocal relationships, as they also provide you with an opportunity to learn about the challenges and expectations of diverse people.

The inclusive leadership mantra

You're now equipped with the Inclusive Leadership Propeller Model© to navigate human differences effectively. It comprises three key inclusive leadership skills (fairness, empathy, and proactivity) and nine basic inclusive leadership habits. The key question you should keep asking yourself in different leadership situations is the FEP question: *How fair, empathetic and proactive am I?* Use it like a mantra. It'll help you identify blind spots and take corrective action.

The Inclusive Leadership Propeller Model ©

The nine basic inclusive leadership habits

Fairness - Are you being fair?

- Identify and challenge biases in yourself and others
- Genuinely follow structured processes instead of simply relying on gut instinct
- Look at metrics and history to identify potential biases and track progress

Empathy - Are you treating others as they'd like to be treated?

- Be curious about people
- Be aware of your impact on others
- Adapt to people's different styles and needs

Proactivity - Are you accelerating positive change?

- Raise awareness about inclusion and diversity
- Reach out to diverse candidates
- Mentor and sponsor diverse people

5

THIRTY QUESTIONS TO ASSESS YOURSELF

"Success doesn't come from what you do occasionally; it comes from what you do consistently."
—Marie Forleo

Now, it's time to find out how inclusive you are and to commit to change.

Assessing yourself

The inclusive leadership self-assessment comprises thirty inclusive leadership habits distributed in seven leadership areas. The thirty habits represent a more detailed and concrete version of the nine basic inclusive leadership habits. For each one of the thirty habits, a real-life example is given so that you can clearly picture the type of behaviour that's expected of you.

Read each habit and answer the question, "How often do you do this?" You have four options; each option gives you a certain number of points: 1 (never), 2 (sometimes), 3 (often), and 4 (always).

This self-assessment allows you to understand your overall competence level, as well as your performance by leadership area and by inclusive leadership skill.

You'll need to do a little bit of math; it'll be easier with a calculator:

- Add all your points to find out your total score that reveals your overall competence level on inclusive leadership: beginner, intermediate, advanced or mastery level.

- Add your points to find out your scores per leadership area (awareness & commitment, communications, hiring & onboarding, talent management & rewards, learning & development, working organisation, working atmosphere), and find your average score per area by dividing your score by the number of questions in each area. This allows you to compare your performance between areas and understand where your strengths and weaknesses are. For example: You scored 13 points in communications. To find your average score, you divide 13 by 4 (the number of questions asked in communications). Your average score is 3.25. You might find out that you have the highest average score in communications and the lowest average score in learning & development. While the average scores are good for comparison between different leadership areas, the scores make it easier to measure your progress over time.

- Add your points to find out your scores per inclusive leadership skill (fairness, empathy, proactivity) and find your average score per skill by dividing your score by the number of questions for each skill. For example: You scored 24 points in empathy. To find your average score, you divide 24 by 8 (the number of questions related to empathy). Your average score is 3. This allows you to compare your performance between skills and understand where your strengths and weaknesses are. You might find out that you have the highest average score in fairness and the lowest average score in empathy. While the average scores are good for comparison between different skills, the scores make it easier to measure your progress over time.

If you feel comfortable, print copies of the self-assessment and ask your direct reports to fill in the assessment anonymously. You'll get a far more accurate picture of how well you're doing.

Building your inclusive leadership action plan

The inclusive leadership action plan template has been designed based on effective habit changing techniques.[58]

Based on the results of your self-assessment, identify the habits that are missing and that are most aligned with your inclusive leadership drivers (exercise done on chapter 2). Example: if engaging your team is one of you inclusive leadership drivers, it's not very helpful to identify habits that relate to hiring. "Asking for feedback about my leadership style" is a habit that would potentially lead to more results in your case.

Becoming an unconsciously competent inclusive leader

At the beginning of your inclusive leadership journey, most probably you are not aware of your own biases or your inability to put yourself in other people's shoes. You don't know what you don't know. That's when you are unconsciously incompetent. Then you become aware of the problem but don't have the skills yet to bring solutions; you become consciously incompetent. Then comes the moment you are aware of the skills and habits you need to develop, but they don't come naturally to you. You need to make an effort. You become consciously competent. The final learning stage is when you become unconsciously competent, i.e., when you naturally behave inclusively in different leadership situations.[59]

To help you reach that stage, you need to create new habits in a systemic way.

Making inclusive leadership habits stick

Research tells us that the easiest way to introduce a new habit in our lives is to:

- Start small. You shouldn't identify more than three inclusive habits at a time.
- Start easy. It's better to focus on your strengths first and gain confidence in your comfortable zones before your tackle more

challenging areas. For instance, if you're already good at hiring inclusively, and hiring is aligned with your inclusive leadership drivers, try to become excellent in hiring before you tackle a leadership area where your scores are lower.

- Follow a three-step process: set a reminder for your new habit (for example, recruiting interviews), practice the habit (for example, ask the same questions in the same order to all candidates every time you're participating in recruiting interviews), and reward yourself (it could be something as simple as congratulating yourself, having a tea break, watching one more episode of your favourite series).

- Go public; tell others what your intentions are. Social pressure influences change positively.

- Read your action plan regularly (or before your reminder). Print it and display it somewhere where it's always in your sight.

- Schedule a regular meeting with someone to check on your progress. It could be a colleague, your manager, an assistant or with yourself. It could be once a month for six months, for example. It depends on the type of habit you chose to practice.

- Stick to your action plan as long as it takes to form your new habit. You know, something becomes a habit when you do it effortlessly.

INCLUSIVE LEADERSHIP SELF-ASSESSMENT

(F)= Fairness habit - (E)= Empathy habit - (P)= Proactivity habit

Awareness & Commitment

INCLUSIVE HABIT	How often do you do this?
1- I make a conscious effort to go beyond first impressions. (F)	1- Never
	2- Sometimes
	3- Often
	4- Always

Example: you're hiring for a manager position. Ahmed is a very good candidate in his 50's. Your first thought is "he's probably too costly for this position". Instead of excluding Ahmed from the recruiting process, you interview him and ask him about his salary expectations. You find out his expectations fit within your budget.

2- I identify and challenge biases in myself and others. (F)	1- Never
	2- Sometimes
	3- Often
	4- Always

Example: you're part of the discussions to decide whether or not to promote Martha, who recently came back from maternity leave. Ludovic, one of your colleagues says "It's not a good idea to promote her right now, she needs time for her baby". You remind your colleagues that if Martha qualifies for the promotion, she should be the one who decides whether it's a good time for her.

3- I look at history and metrics to identify potential biases and track progress. (F)	1- Never
	2- Sometimes
	3- Often
	4- Always

Example: as you want to treat inclusion and diversity like any other business topic, you decide to look at recruitment, promotion and retention rates by gender during every quarterly business review and every annual talent review.

4- I set up inclusion and diversity objectives for myself and for my team. (P)	1- Never
	2- Sometimes
	3- Often
	4- Always

Example: your team has become increasingly international, with team members based in the US, in the UK, in Singapore, and in France. You noticed the communications are not always easy. You decide this year one of your objectives is to train everybody on cross cultural communications.

SCORE	

Communications

INCLUSIVE HABIT	How often do you do this?
5- I share information with and listen to my team members in an equitable way. (F)	1- Never
	2- Sometimes
	3- Often
	4- Always

Example: you realise that during team meetings, the more vocal team members monopolise the conversations. You decide to run meetings in a different way, and give everyone's time to speak at the end of each meeting.

6- I adapt myself to different communication styles and needs. (E)	1- Never
	2- Sometimes
	3- Often
	4- Always

Example: you travel to meet your teams based in Paris. As everybody's is not fluent in English, you avoid speaking too fast and using slang.

7- I encourage people with different opinions and backgrounds (regarding gender, age, ethnicity, nationality, etc.) to share their views. (P)	1- Never
	2- Sometimes
	3- Often
	4- Always

Example: Speranza has a very different thinking style from the team. She's very analytical. The team is more creative. You always make sure she has the opportunity to voice her opinions.

8- I communicate the value of inclusion & diversity. (P)	1- Never
	2- Sometimes
	3- Often
	4- Always

Example: you meet Tony during a job interview. As you're presenting the company to him, you talk about the initiatives you're taking to build an inclusive environment.

SCORE	

Hiring & Onboarding

INCLUSIVE HABIT	How often do you do this?
9- I post job ads whenever I have job vacancies. (F)	1- Never
	2- Sometimes
	3- Often
	4- Always

Example: Maya went to the same University you went to, and would be a good candidate for a position in your team. You contact her and at the same time post a job ad to make sure you reach out to as many qualified candidates as possible outside your network.

10- I follow a structured process when I'm hiring. (F)	1- Never
	2- Sometimes
	3- Often
	4- Always

Example: you're hiring for an engineer role. You ask the same questions, in the same order, to all candidates. You also use assessment grids.

11- I look for a diverse short list of candidates (regarding gender, age, ethnicity, nationality, etc.). (P)	1- Never
	2- Sometimes
	3- Often
	4- Always

Example: you're hiring for a senior manager position. You tell Pedro, the recruiter you're working with, that you want to have a short list with qualified men and women with different ages and backgrounds.

12- I set up diverse panels of interviewers (regarding gender, age, ethnicity, nationality, etc.). (P)	1- Never
	2- Sometimes
	3- Often
	4- Always

Example: you're interviewing people for a role. You don't have women in your team, but to make sure the hiring discussions are balanced, you invite Alice from another department to join the panel of interviewers.

13- I take into account people's special needs during the hiring process and the onboarding. (E)	1- Never
	2- Sometimes
	3- Often
	4- Always

Example: you meet Thomas, a new hire. You ask him if he has everything he needs to get started and whether there are any special accommodation needs you should be aware of to make sure he's comfortable and well equipped.

SCORE	

Talent Management & Rewards

INCLUSIVE HABIT	How often do you do this?
14- I promote people based on objective and verifiable criteria. (based on performance reviews, succession planning, etc.). (F)	1- Never 2- Sometimes 3- Often 4- Always
Example: there's a director position opened. One of your peers, Peter, suggests you should make the proposal to Alan. You say that based on past performance and talent reviews, Julia is more qualified for the job. To make sure she's the best choice, you open up the position to interview other internal and external candidates, including Alan.	
15- I evaluate people's performance based on facts. (F)	1- Never 2- Sometimes 3- Often 4- Always
Example: I avoid taking decisions about people's performance if I'm hungry, tired or in a hurry, as I become more prone to biases under this circumstances.	
16- I provide my team members with clear explanations regarding performance evaluations, promotions and rewards decisions. (F)	1- Never 2- Sometimes 3- Often 4- Always
Example: it's the second time Igor's application for a higher position gets rejected. You meet him to explain clearly to him why he wasn't given the opportunity this time and what he can do to increase his chances of getting a promotion next time.	
17- I check pay levels by gender to ensure there are no gender pay gaps and take corrective action if needed. (F)	1- Never 2- Sometimes 3- Often 4- Always
Example: it's the time of the year you decide who's going to get a pay raise. Before you take any decisions, you check the salary levels by gender. You realize there's no reason why Amanda is getting a lower salary than the rest of the team. You allocate part of your budget to correct the pay gap.	
18- I mentor and sponsor people with different backgrounds (regarding gender, age, ethnicity, nationality, etc.). (P)	1- Never 2- Sometimes 3- Often 4- Always
Example: you realize that all of your "protégés" have always been very similar to you. You find Emilia, a high potential who's very different from you, a woman from a different generation, ethnic and social background, and start supporting her.	
SCORE	

Learning & Development

INCLUSIVE HABIT	How often do you do this?
19- I assign projects and tasks to my team members in an equitable way. (F)	1- Never 2- Sometimes 3- Often 4- Always

Example: there's a strategic European project you need to assign to someone. Before you do it, you review who has been given strategic projects in the past, to make sure you're not always giving developmental opportunities to the same people.

20- I give positive and negative feed-back to my team members in an equitable way. (F)	1- Never 2- Sometimes 3- Often 4- Always

Example: every time a project works well, you congratulate every team member involved in it.

21- I favour knowledge-sharing and team work between people with different backgrounds (regarding gender, age, ethnicity, nationality, etc.). (P)	1- Never 2- Sometimes 3- Often 4- Always

Example: you noticed Karl's not very digital. You decide to pair Karl and Milena, the new graduate, who happens to be very tech savvy and connected. You ask Karl to present the organisation to Milena and ask Milena to support Karl with IT and social media.

22- I ask my team members what motivates them so that I can better engage and support them. (E)	1- Never 2- Sometimes 3- Often 4- Always

Example: During the annual review with Aurelia, you ask her what aspects of the job she likes the most and what her aspirations for the future are.

23- I ask my team members for feedback on the impact of my leadership style in supporting them. (E)	1- Never 2- Sometimes 3- Often 4- Always

You're having the performance reviews with each one of your team members. You ask every single one of them what you could do differently to better support them.

SCORE	

Working Organisation

INCLUSIVE HABIT	How often do you do this?
24- I ask my team members what can be done to improve their work-life integration and together we work on feasible solutions. (P)	1- Never 2- Sometimes 3- Often 4- Always

Example: Mamadou, one of your team members, asks if it's possible to avoid team meetings early in the mornings, as he needs to take his kids to school. You take the opportunity to ask all team members if they have preferences regarding the team meeting time, and reschedule the meeting taking everyone's input into account as much as possible.

25- I avoid calling upon my team members outside regularly scheduled hours of work, during week-ends or on holidays. (E)	1- Never 2- Sometimes 3- Often 4- Always

Example: you enjoy catching up with emails on Sunday evenings. To make sure you don't disturb your colleagues and customers, you use the delayed option so that people only get your messages Monday.

26- When I organise company events, I take into account dietary requirements, major religious festivities dates, and leisure's preferences. (E)	1- Never 2- Sometimes 3- Often 4- Always

Example: you're organising your next leadership team meeting. You make sure you choose a date that is not a major religious festivity.

27- I enquire about my team member's special accommodation needs and I make every effort to take them into account. (E)	1- Never 2- Sometimes 3- Often 4- Always

Example: somebody tells you that one of your colleagues, Nancy, is going to the toilette too often, and suggests she's taking drugs... You have a conversation with Nancy and ask her if she feels comfortable sharing with you what's going on, so that you can support her. You find out she has severe diabetes.

SCORE	

Working Atmosphere

INCLUSIVE HABIT	How often do you do this?
28- I avoid making remarks that could hurt other people's feelings and I speak out when I come across disrespectful remarks or behaviours. (F)	1- Never
	2- Sometimes
	3- Often
	4- Always
Example: you're having a coffee break, and one of your colleagues, Crystal, tells a gay joke. Most people laugh. You tell everyone that the office is not the place to crack gay jokes, we might hurt people's feelings.	
29- In the workplace, I socialise with people with different backgrounds (regarding gender, age, ethnicity, nationality, etc.). (E)	1- Never
	2- Sometimes
	3- Often
	4- Always
Example: once a week, you have lunch with a different colleague.	
30- I favour connections within my team. (P)	1- Never
	2- Sometimes
	3- Often
	4- Always
Example: Monica, an intern, seems a bit lost in her first weeks in the new job. You come to talk to her to see how she's doing. You also ask Dirk to be her buddy and show her around.	
SCORE	

INCLUSIVE LEADERSHIP SELF-ASSESSMENT RESULTS (1)

INCLUSIVE LEADERSHIP COMPETENCE LEVELS

Beginner Score 30-54	Intermediate Score 55-77	Advanced Score 78-100	Mastery Score 101-120
There's a lot of room for improvement. But this is a good start: you know where you stand and how to start your inclusive leadership journey.	You are on the way to becoming an inclusive leader. Keep looking for new ways to give life to inclusion and diversity in everyday situations.	Well done! You're ahead of most people on the inclusive leadership journey. Keep looking for your blind spots.	Congratulations! You're creating a truly inclusive culture, fostering engagement, productivity and innovation in your team. Keep up the good work!

TOTAL SCORE	
COMPETENCE LEVEL	

INCLUSIVE LEADERSHIP SELF-ASSESSMENT RESULTS (2)

BY LEADERSHIP AREA

	Score	Average score
Awareness & Commitment	/4	
Communications	/4	
Hiring and Onboarding	/5	
Talent Management & Rewards	/5	
Learning & Development	/5	
Working Organisation	/4	
Working Atmosphere	/3	

BY INCLUSIVE LEADERSHIP SKILL

	Score	Average score
FAIRNESS	/13	
EMPATHY	/8	
PROACTIVITY	/9	

To find your average score, divide your score by the number in each box. This number corresponds to the number of questions related to each leadership area or inclusive leadership skill.

MY INCLUSIVE LEADERSHIP ACTION PLAN

MY INCLUSIVE LEADERSHIP DRIVERS
#1
#2
#3

INCLUSIVE LEADERSHIP HABITS
HABIT #1 : Reminder: Reward:
HABIT #2 : Reminder: Reward:
HABIT #3 : Reminder: Reward:

Inclusive leadership is a journey, not a destination

Well done! You managed to get to the end of part I.

Don't forget that inclusive leadership is a journey, not a destination; commitment to continuous improvement is key. Reassess yourself regularly, for instance, twice a year. This is a good way to measure your progress and to identify new inclusive leadership habits to adopt, based on your reviewed results.

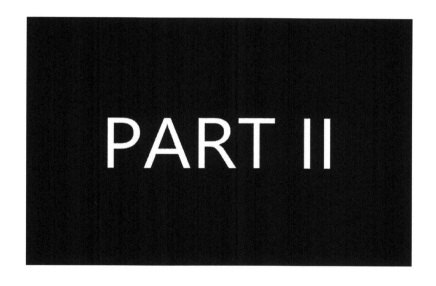

PART II

GOING TO THE NEXT LEVEL

"Make progress one time and it makes you happy.
Make progress day after day, week after week, and it makes
you a champion."
—Greg Werner

Part I gave you a solid foundation to start your inclusive leadership journey in the right direction. You now understand the common inclusion and exclusion mechanisms across differences. You know where you stand, how to identify your inclusive leadership drivers, and how to build your action plan. You have a framework to navigate differences—the Inclusive Leadership Propeller Model ©.

Part II delves into the specific barriers and inclusive leadership habits related to different inclusion and diversity dimensions: **gender, generations, disability, nationality, ethnicity, religion, sexual orientation, and work-life integration**. It offers you a practical application of the Inclusive Leadership Propeller Model ©.

You don't need to read the next chapters in the order that they are displayed. They are independent of each other and self-contained. Feel free to move around and select the different topics according to your own interests and needs.

It might be easier, more rewarding, and more sustainable over time to build on your strengths. I recommend that you first make progress in the areas where you believe you're already good at, and only then tackle the subjects that seem more challenging to you.

6

ACCELERATING GENDER BALANCE

"We cannot all succeed when half of us are held back."
—Malala Youzafsai

Isabelle Kocher
CEO of Engie

Sheryl Sandberg
Chief Operating Officer of
Facebook

Ana Patricia Botín
Executive Chairman of
Santander Group

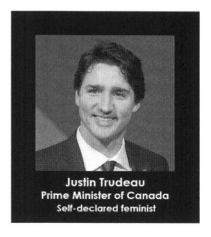

Justin Trudeau
Prime Minister of Canada
Self-declared feminist

Gender balance is not only about women; it's about men as well

Gender balance (or gender diversity) is by far the most high-profile of all inclusion and diversity topics in the corporate world. It's the one in which companies invest the most and the one about which society expectations are the highest. It has the advantage of being a universal theme and is easily measurable.

But it's also a topic that, today, generates a certain fatigue, given the fact that there's a lot of talk about it, but relatively small progress made. According to the World Economic Forum, if we continue to progress at the same pace, we will only achieve gender equality in the year 2186.[60] A McKinsey study showed that only sixteen percent of companies that invest in gender balance see results.[61]

Gender balance is achieved in a team when you have at least forty percent of men and forty percent of women. Gender balance is not only about women; it's about men as well. But women face much more obstacles in the workplace than men. Even in highly feminised functions, men have an advantage. This is known as the "glass escalator" effect, which refers to how men in female-dominated careers, such as public relations, often rise higher and faster than women. On one occasion I was presenting to a human resources team in France. In the room, there were 34 women and six men. All men and only one woman were in management positions. I'm sure you've seen a similar pattern in other female dominated functions.

That said, one of the biggest mistakes in gender balance initiatives is to make it a women's only problem. Men, as the current majority of senior leaders, are the biggest decision makers who can move the needle. If they are not involved, change won't happen.

This chapter gives you the keys to attract, develop, and retain women in a way that's inclusive of men.

WHAT YOU NEED TO KNOW

Three key gender balance challenges

Women tend to face more difficulties to progress in their careers, to be paid less, and to be concentrated in fewer jobs than men.

- **The leaky pipeline**

  Women make up only five percent of CEOs and fourteen percent of executive committees of Fortune 500 companies.[62] Across all industries and countries, the more you climb the corporate ladder, the fewer women you see. It's common to talk about the "glass ceiling," a metaphor used to represent an invisible barrier that keeps women from rising beyond a certain level in a hierarchy. In reality, from the very start of their careers, women face difficulties. Women at entry level are three times less likely than men to be promoted to the next level.[63] And the gaps persist at every transitional point.

- **The gender pay gap**

  Despite abundant legislation in industrialized countries to ensure equal pay, the gender pay gap persists. On average, globally, women earn 23 percent less than man.[64] Some structural factors explain partially the difference: women tend to occupy less well-remunerated positions, less senior roles, and more part-time roles. However, there remains a gap for which no reasonable explanation can be given. And the gender pay gap regarding bonuses tends to be even higher. For instance, in the UK, male traders get double the bonuses of women.[65] Interestingly, one of the highest paid female CEOs in the US, Martine Rothblatt, Chairwoman of United Therapeutics, was born male.[66] Ironically, a financial director once told me that he loved recruiting women because they were cheaper skilled labour.

- **Occupational segregation**

  Women and men tend to be segregated into different industries and types of jobs. For instance, in the US, roughly seventy percent of workers are in occupations that are at least two-thirds single-sex.[67] Women tend to be concentrated in fewer occupations, mostly in clerical, service, and professional occupations. Segregation starts early, with clear distinctions between the degrees chosen by men and by women. "Traditional career paths" offer women less of a choice, and deprive whole sectors of female talents, as it is the case with STEM (Science, Technology, Engineering, and Mathematics) sectors. In addition, once in corporations, even women who start their careers in less traditionally female roles will tend to go into support roles as they progress in their careers.

Ten key barriers for gender balance

The barriers to achieving more gender balance are related to biases, to the work culture and organisation, to women's internal barriers and lack of leadership support.

Biases

- **The pro-male bias**

  Male performance is often overestimated compared to female performance. A meta-analysis of 111 studies from 1970 to 2012 with data from over 22,000 participants[68] showed that there was a preference for men across industries and occupations in hiring, promotion, compensation, competency, and job performance. There was a pro-male bias across all jobs, especially those considered 'male-dominated.' But there was no pro-female bias for stereotypically 'female' occupations. The pro-male bias can be hard to pinpoint at times. I've seen an organisation where succession planning seemed quite gender balanced at first glance. But when you looked closer, most women were not considered "ready now" for a new position, whereas most men were.

- **The motherhood penalty**

  Many studies show that the pushback—or "motherhood penalty"—women experience when they have kids is the strongest gender bias. Motherhood triggers assumptions that a woman is less competent, less committed, and less available to her career.[69] A survey in the UK showed that nearly half of working women are nervous about telling their boss they are pregnant.[70] And eleven percent of women in the UK are pushed out of their jobs after maternity leave.[71] In France, another survey showed that 37 percent of women between 30 and 39 years were asked during a job interview whether they were planning to have children.[72] The "motherhood penalty" has been proven again and again but more recently researchers have also noted a "fatherhood bump". Experiments from Cornell University showed that women with children were 50 per cent less likely to get a response from an employer and were offered salaries of around $11,000 less than women without children. Men with children were slightly more likely than any other applicant to get a call back for interview and were offered salaries of around $2000 more.[73]

- **The "think leader think male" bias**

  Men and women tend to associate leadership with more masculine traits such as strength, assertiveness, confidence. And men and women don't judge the same traits in a woman as positively. An assertive woman tends to be viewed as "bossy." I've observed several discussions during talent management reviews where women were criticised for being too "aggressive." I've rarely seen this remark made about men under review. At the same time, a woman exhibiting a typically feminine leadership style, more collaborative, asking more questions rather than giving orders, will be considered too "soft" for a leadership role. Studies also show that the more powerful a man is, the more likeable he becomes. Whereas for women, the opposite is true—the more powerful a woman becomes, the less likeable. Sheryl Sandberg has described this phenomenon very well in her acclaimed book, titled *Lean In*. For these reasons, women tend to be appointed less to leadership positions.

- **The benevolence bias**

  The benevolence bias consists in associating women with vulnerability and the need for protection. This has at least two negative implications for women's career progression: First, they tend to be given fewer stretch assignments and positions. Typically, women with small children tend not to be considered for international assignments, as managers assume this would be too challenging for them. Second, women get less constructive feedback as managers fear the emotional reactions of women. It's true that, in general, women tend to be more emotional than men. A study showed that women shed tears as much as eight times more often than men. And when women cried, the duration of crying was three times longer.[74] But this is not a sign of weakness. It's mostly a result of socialisation, as women are given more permission to cry than men.

Work culture and organisation

- **Difficulties in managing work-life**

  Society's expectations are not the same on men and women regarding their roles raising children, carrying out household chores or looking after ageing parents. Things are progressing, but around the world, women still spend two to ten times more time on unpaid care work than men.[75] A McKinsey study also showed that about half of the women tend to be both primary breadwinners and caregivers, while most men are primary breadwinners, but not primary caregivers.[76] The double burden women face is clearly a reality. Therefore, the "anytime anywhere" culture and the lack of flexible working options have a disproportionately negative impact on women.

- **Ordinary sexism**

  Sadly, ordinary sexism is still a key obstacle for gender balance in the workplace. Such behaviours are particularly strong in male-dominated industries. They make women feel like outsiders and discourage them to both apply to jobs or remain in such environments. I've run several focus groups in male-dominated companies. Women often share stories about how they feel disrespected and how ashamed they are to talk about it. A typical thing they say: *You get used to it until you get fed up with it and leave.* Often male colleagues don't even realise how inappropriate some behaviours may be. In France, a study showed that eighty percent of women have experienced sexist behaviours at work.[77] According to a UK survey, the most common sexist behaviours women must put up with are: being expected to make the tea (43 percent of surveyed), enduring sexual innuendos (38 percent) or having appearance or clothing commented on (33 percent).[78] Some team cultures that are not exactly sexist can put off women when they are too masculine, too competitive, with rough language, and ongoing banter. I've seen this happening in a sales team in Norway, for example.

Women's internal barriers

- **Lack of confidence**

  Several studies show that women tend to be less confident in themselves than men, even if they have similar ambitions to progress in their careers.[79] For instance, women tend to apply for jobs only when they fulfil 100 percent of requirements, whereas men apply for jobs even if they only fulfil 60 percent of requirements.[80] In a group of women and men with similar performances, the women will tend to under evaluate themselves, whereas the men will tend to over evaluate themselves. Women tend to blame themselves when they fail and credit external circumstances when they succeed, whereas men tend to do the opposite. Due to this confidence gap, women also tend to negotiate their salaries four times less than men, and when they do, they ask for thirty percent less.[81] Self-censorship is one of the many negative implications of this lack of confidence that's only reinforced by the scarcity of female role models at leadership positions and in traditionally male-dominated industries.

- **The good girl syndrome**

  Women have been conditioned at school, more than men, that a good job is automatically rewarded, something called *The good girl syndrome*. While this approach works well at school, it doesn't work in corporations. To progress in your career, it's not enough to do a good job. Others need to know what you're capable of. Women, compared with men, have less of the attitude and the network required to succeed in this type of environment. Women tend to be less comfortable than men communicating about their accomplishments. They fear being viewed as bragging and self-promoting. They also tend to spend less time networking than men, as they don't view networking as necessary and they also have less time, given their double burden. For all these reasons, highly political corporate environments that demand strong politics skills, and where invisible networks are very influential, tend to be less favourable to women.

Lack of leadership support

- **The perception gap**

  Men and women don't share the same vision of gender equality. Overall, men tend to underestimate the difficulties faced by women and the benefits of having more gender diversity. A study showed that 93 percent of women believe that "women have more difficulties reaching to top management positions," compared to only 58 percent of men.[82] Other study found that only 24 percent of male board members believe having diverse boards increase company performance, compared to 89 percent of female board members.[83] A survey in the high tech industry found that while, for men, the key gender diversity barrier was the classic pipeline excuse, *There are no women to recruit*, for women, unconscious bias was the key barrier.[84] The less men are aware of their male privilege and the difficulties women face, the less supportive they are of gender diversity measures. If a man fails, will he ever be told that *it's because you're a man*? Most probably not, and this is male privilege. Because many women are reminded of their gender when they fail, amongst other things. Men happen to be the majority of senior leaders, those with the power to change the status quo. For change to happen, more men need to champion gender equality. When Madonna received the Women of the Year Award during the Billboard Women in Music 2016, she gave a truly enlightening speech about the challenges she faced as a woman; check it out. [85]

- **The lack of knowledge about what to do**

  Even when leaders are aware of the barriers faced by women, and convinced of the benefits to promote gender balance, often they don't know what to do. A McKinsey study showed that 49 percent of managers don't know what to do to improve gender diversity.[86] That's one of the most common questions I'm asked by male leaders who want to promote gender balance: "What can I do to move the needle?" "What am I doing wrong?"

WHAT YOU NEED TO DO

Reflect

- Is your team gender balanced at different hierarchical levels?
- Does your team reflect the gender diversity of your customers?
- Are you good at attracting, developing, rewarding and retaining both men and women?
- Are you good at engaging both men and women?
- Is your team culture gender bilingual, i.e., friendly for both men and women?
- How would your team members answer these questions about you?

- Would men and women have similar views?

If, upon reflection, you think you're doing well, CONGRATULATIONS! If you feel there's a lot of room for improvement, no problem. Either way, the Inclusive Leadership Propeller Model © will help you improve your ability to navigate gender differences.

Commit

Find below the specific inclusive leadership habits applied to gender balance:

- Don't take them in isolation. They reinforce and complement the inclusive leadership basic habits you've seen in PART I of this book.
- Don't get overwhelmed. Ask yourself: *What's the one thing I could do differently moving forward?* Then review your inclusive leadership action plan based on this additional information.
- Work-life integration is key for achieving gender balance. You'll find the inclusive leadership habits related to it in the chapter "Supporting work-life integration."

Remember all the great things that gender balance will help you to get: a broader talent pool, more creative ideas, better decision-making, and a better understanding of your customer's needs, amongst others. The effort to make progress is well worth it.

Practice

Once you're clear on the habits you want to integrate into your life, start practicing them. When they become second nature to you, review your commitments, add new habits, and keep going. Inclusive leadership is a journey, not a destination.

Twelve inclusive leadership habits to improve gender balance

Fairness - Are you being fair?

- **Identify and challenge gender biases**

   Challenge yourself and others for considering a woman too "soft" or too "tough," for associating a typical feminine leadership style with weakness, for excluding a woman from opportunities with the intention to protect her. Challenge gender stereotypes, even if they are positive about women, such as "I prefer to hire women because they pay more attention to details." Such stereotypes tend to segregate women in certain roles. Ask yourself, *Would the treatment be the same if it was a man?* Challenge others when they tend to interrupt women during meetings (*manterrupting*) or take credit for their ideas.

- **Respond when you see ordinary sexist behaviours taking place**

   Such as colleagues asking a female colleague to serve tea, to take notes, borderline comments about women's appearance, etc. Your behaviour has a positive impact not only on women but on all men who disapprove of sexist behaviours.

- **Post job ads as much as possible**

   This allows you to mitigate the influence of affinity biases from internal, invisible networks, which tend to be male-dominated, especially when it comes to more senior management positions. This also allows you to find out women's career expectations, as they tend to be less vocal about them than men.

- **Check salary, pay raise, and bonus levels by gender**

   Be careful when you recruit, in order to make salary offers that won't create or strengthen any gender pay gaps in your team. Use every pay raise season as an opportunity to ensure that there are no unjustified gender pay gaps, and take corrective action if needed. If you're not doing anything to intentionally prevent the gender pay gap, most probably you're having one.

- **Look at history and data by gender**

  Do you tend to hire, promote, or evaluate positively more men than women, or vice-versa? Are you engaging and retaining men and women in the same way? Is your talent pipeline gender balanced? Checking data regularly, particularly during talent management reviews, can help you spot any gender biases you might be unaware of.

Empathy – Are you treating others as they'd like to be treated?

- **Make your job adds gender neutral**

  Particularly in male-dominated industries, job descriptions tend to use male-coded words that put off female candidates. Example: "We're a dominant engineering firm" is male-coded, while "We're a community of engineers" is more gender neutral. You can review your job adds using free tools on the internet such as the "gender decoder."[87] You should also make a clear distinction between core skills and additional skills. This will help you attract women who tend to apply only when they fulfil most of the job requirements.

- **Welcome maternity**

  Make life easier for working mothers and aspiring working mothers. This includes celebrating pregnancy announcements. I've seen managers who complained openly about women leaving on maternity, without realising the negative impact on women in their team, particularly young women planning to have a baby. You can also meet women before and after maternity/parental leave to clarify expectations around the work organisation and agree on the way to keep them posted on events and career opportunities while they are away.

- **Boost the confidence of women around you**

  We've seen that the confidence gap is a reality for many women. So, encourage them to speak up, to accept stretch assignments, give them credit. I met an American human resources director who was very good at assigning tasks to team members, particularly when they didn't feel capable of it, and these tended to be his female direct reports. Also, be aware of the impact of the gender confidence gap on performance reviews, particularly if they are based on self-assessments. This practice favours those with higher self-confidence, and they tend to be men. A German human resources director in the construction industry once told me that she was observing annual performance reviews in her company. She saw the few women directors starting their reviews, highlighting what they could have done better, while the men directors kicked off the conversations, boasting about their accomplishments. Curiously, those women had better results than most men in that organisation.

- **Support work-life integration**
  This includes being open to flexible working without penalising those who benefit from it. Read the chapter on work-life integration to find out more about it.

Proactivity – Are you accelerating positive change?

- **Show visible support to gender diversity initiatives**
  Participate in women's networks and gender diversity events (common around March the 8th, the international women's day). If there's nothing going on in your company, consider taking the lead. You can also use every opportunity to raise the awareness of male colleagues about the challenges and benefits of gender balance.

- **Look for gender diverse shortlists of candidates**
  This is an effective rule to force you to look for qualified female candidates who you might have otherwise overlooked. This also works if you're trying to increase the proportion of men in your team. Of course, final decisions must always be based on skills and competence. Research tells us that having at least two women in a shortlist, instead of just one, increases massively your probability of hiring qualified female candidates.

- **Mentor women**

  Mentor women so that they can better understand and navigate the unwritten rules of the political business game. If you're a man, this is also an opportunity for you to understand women's challenges and expectations. You can join official existing mentorship programs in your company. Or you can informally meet with your mentees, agreeing on a cadence of meetings.

- **Sponsor women**

  This means advocating for their advancement when they are not in the room. Several studies point at sponsorship as the key accelerator of gender balance. A McKinsey study looking at the "secret" of women who made it into the leadership ranks found that ninety percent of them had significant sponsorship.[88]

The Inclusive Leadership Propeller Model ©

Twelve inclusive leadership habits to accelerate gender balance

Fairness - Are you being fair?

- Identify an challenge gender biases
- Respond when you see ordinary sexist behaviours taking place
- Check salary, pay raise, and bonus levels by gender
- Look at history and data by gender

Empathy – Are you treating others as they'd like to be treated?

- Make your job adds gender neutral
- Welcome maternity
- Boost the confidence of women around you
- Support work-life integration

Proactivity – Are you accelerating positive change?

- Show visible support to gender diversity initiatives
- Look for gender diverse shortlists of candidates
- Mentor women
- Sponsor women

7

MANAGING MULTIPLE GENERATIONS

"Each generation imagine itself to be more intelligent than
the one that went before it, and wiser than the one that
comes after it."
—George Orwell

Arran Rice
Internet Entrepreneur
Started his first business at 12

Malala Yousafzai
Activist for female education
Youngest Nobel prize laureate ever

Barbara Beskind
Tech-designer
Started her career at 89 years old

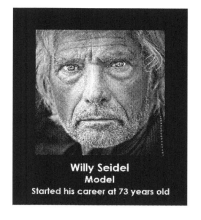

Willy Seidel
Model
Started his career at 73 years old

Four to five generations working together will become increasingly common

Managing multiple generations has become a very trendy topic. A whole consulting industry has developed around it. Some even talk about *generational hysteria*. The millennials, or the generation Y, those born between 1980 and 1996, attract a lot of attention. Indeed, they are the most studied generation ever. Many articles, books and ted talks can be found about them as if they were a new species.[89] I post every day on social media, and my posts about millennials are much more viewed, liked, and shared than any other posts.

However, there is a lot of controversy regarding the empirical evidence of significant differences between generations. And if there are differences, are they due to generational differences, age differences, or differences in career stage? Generational conflicts have always existed; is there anything new about today's generational tensions?

What's true is that four to five generations working together will become increasingly commonplace. With longer life spans and the rise or abolishment of the retirement age in many countries, we'll tend to extend our work lives. At the age of fifty, we could have one-third of our career ahead of us.

Let's give a closer look at myths and realities about generational diversity. The key objective is to help you understand generational similarities and differences so that you can build bridges, rather than walls, between people and create an inclusive culture where people of all ages can succeed.

WHAT YOU NEED TO KNOW

Key definitions

A generation is defined as *all of the people born and living at about the same time, regarded collectively.*[90] There is no consensus about where exactly a generation starts and finishes. Roughly, here are the birth periods of existing generations:

Veterans	Baby-Boomers	Gen X	Gen Y	Gen Z	Gen Alpha
1928 -1945	1946 - 1964	1965 - 1979	1980 - 1996	1997 – 2009	2010 - ?

When do you stop being young? When do you start being old? There is no consensus here either. It depends on your culture, on the type of work you do, on your industry, on different country legislations… For instance, on average in Europe, people consider that you stop being young at the age of forty and start being old at 62. But there are differences between countries. In the UK, the overall perception is that youth stops at 35, whereas in Greece, it stops at 52.[91] Thirty years old might be an old age for a footballer, and a very young one if you're a senior executive. I was once running a focus group in the Netherlands. In the room, people kept talking about how difficult it was for older employees to feel valued. When I asked them what they considered *old*, they told me forty years old!

The generational divide myth

Most recent research suggests that there are more similarities than differences across the generations. When differences exist, they are more linked to age and career stage than to generations. Those were, for instance, the conclusions of three major studies:

- An Oxford Economics report commissioned by SAP "SAP Workforce 2020" that surveyed 2,700 employees and 2,700 executives in 27 countries.[92]

- The IBM Institute for Business Value multigenerational report, titled *Myths, Exaggerations, and Uncomfortable Truths: The Real Story behind Millennials in the Workplace,* that surveyed 1,784 employees from organizations across 12 countries and 6 industries.

- A meta-analysis published in the Journal of Business and Psychology that reviewed 265 articles based on reliable empirical research covering nearly 20,000 workers.[93]

We all want the same things (income, purpose, to feel valued) just in slightly different ways.[94] And predictions of generational conflict in the workplace are often based on anecdotal information.[95]

Three trends affecting all generations

- **New skills will be needed in the future**
  By 2021, over one-third of skills (35 percent) considered important in today's workforce will have changed.[96] Many jobs will disappear, and new types of jobs will be created. Futurist Thomas Frey predicts that by 2030, about fifty percent of all jobs on the planet will not exist anymore.[97]

- **The number of jobs in a lifetime is increasing**
  The average worker currently holds ten different jobs before age forty, and this number is projected to grow.[98] This means that employee retention standards are evolving.

- **Employees have higher expectations regarding work-life integration**
  For different reasons (to have a social life, to care for children or older parents, to volunteer, etc.), employees from different generations are looking for more flexibility. Workplace flexibility is ranked by 75 percent of employees as the top benefit they look for in an employer.[99]

Digital natives versus digital immigrants

There's one real key difference that can be found between Millennials/Gen Z and the previous generations: they are digital natives. The rest of us, including myself, are digital immigrants, i.e., we were brought up before the widespread use of digital technology. The technological landscape has particularly influenced the way digital natives communicate (stronger use of social media and technological devices), relate to authority (less respect for status—as on the internet, everyone has a voice), and expect feedback (they are more used to immediate feedback, as reactions on the net are instantaneous). These differences in attitude can sometimes cause intergenerational misunderstandings.

Differences based on career stage

The reality is, we look for different things at different stages of our careers.[100] That was also the key finding of an event I organised on "How to engage multiple generations" at the time I was working for Coca-Cola Enterprises. All business units had analysed their metrics by age, ran focus groups with different generations, and presented their analysis during a conference with external participation from academia and other companies (EY, Sodexo, Danone, and Acciona).

- Generation Z members are currently exploring vocational preferences, don't have many outside obligations, place a lot of importance on having a sociable life and fun.
- Generation Y members are establishing themselves in a secure niche and looking for advancement. They tend to have a social life just as important as their careers but are starting to found their families.
- Generation X members are aiming to maintain their career achievements and are often responsible for caring for both elders and children alongside their work.
- Baby boomers and veterans are more focused on making a living and expanding their sources of satisfaction.

Five key barriers for generational inclusion

- **Age discrimination**

  Age is the main cause of discrimination in Europe, more than sex or race.[101] It can be felt particularly by older people when applying for jobs or promotions, and in their access to training. For instance, in France, a CV testing found that a CV by a 48 years old man, identical to a CV of a 28 years old man, receives seven times fewer calls for interviews.[102] Only one-third of employees between 55 and 64 are trained, compared with half of those between 25 and 54 years old.[103] Yet research shows that roughly 80 percent of employees of all ages want to keep learning.[104] I worked for a Belgium company where employee's perception was that if you hadn't become a manager at forty years old, there was no way you could ever become one. The data analysis confirmed their perception, as no forty plus first-time managers had been nominated in previous years.

- **High unemployment rates of youth**

  In 2014, the global youth (those below 25) unemployment rate was 13 percent, more than twice the global rate of unemployment.[105] This is due to lack of experience, the mismatch between the skills that youngsters have and the vacancies that employers want to fill, and precarious jobs offered to youth. Germany, which has a relatively low level of youth unemployment, places a lot of emphasis on high-quality vocational courses, apprenticeships, and links with industry.[106]

- **Widespread age stereotyping**

  Age stereotyping is so pervasive that people are less inclined to challenge them, and even internalise them. So many times, I hear people saying "I'm too old for this or I'm too young for that." Many people believe and say out loud that older people are not dynamic, are costly, are more resistant to change, learn less and perform less. Older people also complain about younger people in stereotypical terms, such as "They are entitled, they lack respect, they are not committed, etc." The attention that generational studies attracted also legitimised, to some extent, generational stereotyping.

- **The digital divide**

  As I mentioned earlier, the key difference between the millennials and Gen Z and previous generations is the fact that they are digital natives. The digital revolution affects everyone, and younger generations have an advantage over older generations in this respect. It's important to acknowledge the different digital skills level in a team, although, of course, individuals are unique and you'll find many individuals from older generations perfectly tech savvy. In some cases, discomfort might come from the fact that the established order is turned upside down, as older employees depend on younger employees to understand how to use technology.

- **Tension between younger managers and older employees**

  Increasingly, younger employees manage older team members. This can lead to tension on both sides. At times, there is a feeling of: *Why am I being bossed around by someone without a lot of experience?* On the other hand, the younger person may be insecure and wonder: *How do I do this?* I once met a senior leader who confessed to me that he had never, in his entire career, hired an employee older than himself. He wanted to avoid the discomfort of managing somebody older. He was only 44 years old.

Three myths about employees who are fifty years old and above

- **They cost more**

  Studies show that eighty percent employees who are fifty years old and above are willing to review their salary expectations.[107] This is the case particularly when they are changing careers.

- **They are not flexible**

  Studies show that ninety percent of employees who are fifty years old and above are willing to change jobs.[108]

- **They will leave the organisation soon**

  Employees around fifty years old still have one-third of their careers ahead of. And they tend to be less volatile than younger employees.

WHAT YOU NEED TO DO

Reflect

- Is your team multigenerational?
- Does your team reflect the age diversity of your customers?
- Are you good at attracting, developing, and retaining people of all ages?
- Are you good at engaging people of all ages?
- How would your team members answer these questions about you?
- Would people of different generations have similar views?

If, upon reflection, you think you're doing well, CONGRATULATIONS! If you feel there's a lot of room for improvement, no problem. Either way, the Inclusive Leadership Propeller Model © will help you improve your ability to navigate generational differences.

Commit

Find below the specific inclusive leadership habits applied to generational diversity:

- Don't take them in isolation. They reinforce and complement the inclusive leadership basic habits you've seen in PART I of this book.
- Don't get overwhelmed. Ask yourself: *What's the one thing I could do differently moving forward?* Then review your inclusive leadership action plan based on this additional information.
- Work-life integration is key across generations. You'll find the inclusive leadership habits related to it in the chapter "Supporting work-life integration."

Remember all the great things that effectively leading people of different generations can bring you: greater engagement, greater productivity, and a better understanding of your customer's needs, amongst others. The effort to make progress is well worth it.

Practice

Once you're clear on the habits you want to integrate into your life, start practicing them. When they become second nature to you, review your commitments, add new habits, and keep going. Inclusive leadership is a journey, not a destination.

Twelve inclusive leadership habits to manage multiple generations

Fairness - Are you being fair?

- **Identify and challenge generational biases**

  Respond when you think or hear things like "He's too old to do this…" or "She's too young to do that…" Challenge common associations such as *Young and dynamic,* or common negative remarks such as *Young people are so disrespectful nowadays.* Encourage people to move beyond generalisations and consider the individual. Generational stereotyping can be as harmful as gender or racial stereotyping, or any other type of stereotyping.

- **Develop the skills of all employees, irrespective of age**

  In this changing world, everybody needs to constantly learn new skills. Favour job rotation for all. Encourage older team members to go on training, even if they don't volunteer. Acknowledge gaps in digital skills and offer training or coaching for those who need it, whatever age they are. Make sure the training you're offering uses different channels (virtual, face-to-face) so that it appeals to people with different learning preferences.

- **Look at history and data per age**

  Do you tend to hire, promote, train or positively evaluate people from a certain age? Are you engaging and retaining people of different ages? Look at data regularly, once a year at least. This will help you identify biases you might be unaware of. On one occasion

I was presenting the results of an inclusion and diversity assessment to a leadership team in Sweden, and they couldn't believe their eyes when I showed them that performance rates were consistently lower for older employees, with no reason.

Empathy – Are you treating others as they'd like to be treated?

- **Ask your team members what their career aspirations are, and support them accordingly**

  Don't assume that older people gave up progressing and want to become tutors, or that younger people want to get a promotion as quickly as possible. Find out which changes people are looking for and, together, explore possibilities vertically and horizontally.

- **Flex your way to give feedback**

  Find out: what are people's favourite way to receive feedback and how often? Some people might need more frequent feedback while their work is still in progress; others might be happier with less monitoring.

- **Use a variety of communication styles**

  Ask people which communication channels (phone, text, email, social media, etc.) and frequency they prefer and adapt your communication style where possible.

- **Improve the workplace ergonomics**

  If you're managing people with physically demanding jobs, improving the workplace ergonomics for everyone will help you keep people on board as they grow old.

- **Support work-life integration**

  We've seen that at different career stages, people want more flexibility for different reasons. Read the chapter on work-life integration to find out how to improve work-life integration.

Proactivity – Are you accelerating positive change?

- **Build multi-generational teams**

  When putting together a working group, mingle people from different generations if possible. When hiring, ask yourself, *Is there any generational gap in my team?* Post job ads using traditional media, as well as new channels, so that you can attract a variety of profiles. And place sufficient value on the experience and knowledge people gain, as well as on formal qualifications, so that you don't overlook older candidates.

- **Promote cross-generational reverse mentoring**

  Pair employees from different generations to learn from each other. This can be particularly useful during onboarding, but not only. Reverse mentoring helps younger employees to acquire the social skills to navigate the workplace and employees who need to develop their digital skills to progress.

- **Raise your team's awareness about the impact of the digital revolution on behaviours**

  This is a powerful way to increase collaboration across generations. It can be eye-opening to digital immigrants to understand why digital natives tend to have a different way to relate to authority (in a non-hierarchical way, given the democratic nature of internet where everybody has a voice), to expect feedback (frequently, even if the work is still in progress), and to communicate (intense use of text and social media). Avoid presentations that caricature generational characteristics stating that "The baby-boomers are loyal; the Gen x are ambitious; the millennials are entitled" and so on. They're not useful and can be harmful.

- **Organise multigenerational social events**

  Having fun together is a great way to get to know each other at the individual level and overcome generational barriers. This can be particularly useful in your team if there are age groups that don't interact or generational tensions. You'll also make people at the beginning of their careers happier, as they tend to be looking for more fun in the workplace.

The Inclusive Leadership Propeller Model ©

Twelve inclusive leadership habits
to manage multiple generations

Fairness - Are you being fair?

- Identify and challenge generational biases
- Develop the skills of all employees, irrespective of age
- Look at history and data per age

Empathy – Are you treating others as they'd like to be treated?

- Ask your team members what their career aspirations are and support them accordingly
- Flex your way to give feedback
- Use a variety of communication styles
- Improve the workplace ergonomics
- Support work-life integration

Proactivity – Are you accelerating positive change?

- Build multi-generational teams
- Promote cross-generational reverse mentoring
- Raise your team awareness about the impact of the digital revolution on behaviours
- Organise multigenerational social events

8

PROMOTING DISABILITY INCLUSION

"Disability is the inability to see ability."
—Vikas Khanna

Dorine Bourneton
Acrobatic pilot
Has paraplegia

Sir Richard Branson
Founder Virgin Group
Has dyslexia

Abraham Lincoln
16th President of the USA
Had depression

Anna Lawson
Law Professor
Visually impaired

People with disabilities are the fastest growing minority group

People's attitudes towards disability inclusion can be inconsistent. Some people feel sorry for people with disabilities and admire them for their courage. They see their inclusion as a charitable act and a moral imperative. However, they fail to see the abilities disabled people bring to the workplace.

Disability inclusion can also generate anxiety. On the one hand, the sight and thought of disabilities remind some people of their fragile condition, of the fact that anything can happen to anyone at any time. On the other hand, they don't know how to behave in the presence of people with disabilities. So, they prefer to avoid the topic, consciously or unconsciously.

But this isn't a topic you can afford to ignore: people with disabilities are said to be the fastest-growing minority group.[109] This is due to the aging societies as well as improved medical treatment helping babies to survive and people to live with long-term health problems. Right now, many of your customers and employees already have some form of disability.

Several countries have also established quotas to encourage companies to employee people with disabilities (Germany, Spain, Brazil, France, etc.) and penalize financially organisations who fail to reach such quotas.

Disability inclusion can be a highly technical subject that involves team work with different stakeholders (medical services, governmental institutions, etc.). But, as an inclusive leader, you don't have to be a disability expert to increase the well-being, engagement, and productivity of people with disabilities in your team, while improving the work environment for non-disabled people. Here's what you need to know and do.

WHAT YOU NEED TO KNOW

Key definitions

A disability is an impairment that has a substantial effect on a person's ability to do normal daily activities.[110] A disability can be:

- Physical (for example, missing limbs), sensory (for example, hearing loss), intellectual (for example, Down syndrome), mental (for example, schizophrenia), learning (for example, dyslexia) or a health condition (for example, severe diabetes).

- Permanent or temporary (for example, a temporary impairment that is the result of an accident).

- Visible (for example, using a wheelchair) or invisible (for example, epilepsy). Eighty percent of disabilities are invisible.[111]

- Of high, medium or low severity.

- Congenital or not. 78 percent of people acquire their impairment after they were born.[112]

Reasonable adjustments

The main barrier to performance at work is not the disability itself, but certain features of the work that could otherwise be modified. A "reasonable adjustment" or "accommodation" is a change or adaptation to the working environment that has the effect of removing or minimising the impact of the individual's impairment. Examples: flexible working patterns, extra time during selection tests, ergonomic seating, anti-glare screens, ramps and rails, adapted telephones for hearing impairment. Although eighty percent of companies fear the costs related to reasonable adjustments, most accommodations can be made at low or no cost.[113] In the UK, the most common accommodation is modified working hours.[114] Often adjustments for one individual can benefit whole teams. I've seen a company that soundproofed an open space to improve the working environment for one employee who had a hearing impairment. The other 200 employees working in the open space appreciated the change.

Key disability facts:

- **The proportion of people with disabilities**

  Twenty percent of people in America and 26 percent of people in Europe experience some form of disability.[115] The prevalence of disability rises with age: for example, in the UK, seven percent of children are disabled compared to sixteen percent of adults of working age (16−64 years), and 42 percent of adults over 65.[116]

- **Disability discrimination**

  In Europe, twenty percent of people with disabilities feel unfairly treated because of their disability.[117] Only 47 percent of disabled people are employed compared to 72 percent of non-disabled people.[118] The top three types of workplace discrimination identified by employed adults with a disability are: being given fewer responsibilities, not being promoted, and being refused a job.[119]

- **Trending topics**

  The World Health Organisation has predicted that depression will be the leading cause of disability by 2020.[120] In France, mental disabilities are already the first cause of sick leaves.[121]

Six key barriers for disability inclusion:

- **A caricatural vision of people with disabilities**

  Most people associate disabilities with highly severe, permanent, congenital, and visible impairments—such as being in a wheelchair. As you could see above, the disability universe is very diverse. In fact, only two percent of disabled people are in wheelchairs and eighty percent of disabilities are invisible.[122] People also think that certain roles cannot be fulfilled by a person with a disability, or that you need to create specific roles for disabled people. In reality, it always depends on the person and the role. You can have paraplegia and be an acrobatic pilot, like the French pilot Dorine Bourneton. I've known a receptionist who was blind. I've met managers whose first reaction to my question about disabilities was: "It's impossible to have a wheelchair in our construction work site" or "we have no roles for the disabled." The irony is that, in many working sites, there are workers with back problems that could qualify as disabilities. This caricatural vision prevents people from even considering starting to tackle the subject. At the end of the day, most of us actually have some kind of disability, don't we? Is anyone reading this wearing glasses?[123]

- **Negative biases**

Eight out of ten people in the UK state that there is a lot of prejudice towards disabled people.[124] People often believe that disabled people are less productive, are slower to perform tasks, more absent from work and unfit for managerial roles. 75 percent of people think of disabled people as needing to be cared for some or most of the time.[125] This suggests a degree of 'benevolent bias' impacting, in particular, the career development opportunities of people with disabilities. Interestingly, research shows that the higher the level of education, the stronger the negative biases towards disabled people.[126] Yet, surveys also show that 93 percent of employers are satisfied with their disabled employees.[127]

- **Lack of team support**

When a person in a team has a known disability, there might be the fear within the team of a lack of equity in the distribution of tasks, and of team performance decrease. I just came back from a manufacturing facility where this was a major problem. However, a survey showed that eighty percent of employees working with a disabled person didn't feel any additional charge of work or decrease in performance.[128] Disabled individuals sometimes feel the pressure to do better than non-disabled peers—almost in order to justify their existence and to prove that they are not a burden. Disabled individuals might also feel isolated when colleagues avoid contact, not knowing how to behave in the presence of a disabled new colleague or someone returning to work after an illness or an accident.

- **Difficulties to disclose**

  It's difficult to disclose, because it can be difficult to accept in the first place, that we have a disability. Then, given all the negative stigma associated with disabilities, people with invisible disabilities fear the consequences of disclosing it. In France, for instance, 49 percent of people don't disclose their disabilities.[129] The problem is, if you don't disclose, you can't get financial support in case you need any adjustments. And your behaviours might be misunderstood as well. I've seen the case of an intern who had a hearing impairment and didn't mention it. As she preferred written communications and didn't interact, her manager thought she wasn't enjoying her job experience and didn't propose her a job. Surveys show that people with invisible disabilities are less satisfied at work than people with visible disabilities.[130] Hiding a disability can be stressful, just like being *in the closet* for gays, lesbians, and bisexuals. And dangerous. I met a worker who developed a temporary eye problem. He could barely see anything, but kept coming to work and said nothing to his manager—for fear of losing his job. People who disclose their disabilities and get management support, free up emotional energy and become more productive.

- **Real and perceived physical barriers**

  A common reason given for not hiring people with disabilities is the fear of costly special facilities.[131] In fact, in 85 percent of cases, people with disabilities don't need adjustments to their working environment.[132] When adjustments are needed, often there's a lack of in-house expertise on how to adapt or how to get government subsidies for such adjustments.

- **Lack of formal qualifications**

  Disabled adults, who were born with their disabilities, are nearly three times as likely as non-disabled adults to have no formal qualifications.[133] This is a real obstacle to hiring disabled people, and the reason why many proactive companies support disabled people with specific training and apprentice programs.

WHAT YOU NEED TO DO

Reflect

- How open are you to recruiting a disabled person?
- Do you have disabled people in your team that you know of?
- Are you providing them with the most supportive working conditions?
- Can they progress as much as other team members?
- Is there a chance that people with a hidden disability or a health issue feel afraid to tell you about it?
- How would your team members answer these questions about you?
- Particularly your disabled team members?

If, upon reflection, you think you're doing well, CONGRATULATIONS! If you feel there's a lot of room for improvement, no problem. Either way, the Inclusive Leadership Propeller Model © will help you improve your ability to promote disability inclusion.

Commit

Find below the specific inclusive leadership habits applied to disability inclusion:

- Don't take them in isolation. They reinforce and complement the inclusive leadership basic habits you've seen in PART I of this book.
- Don't get overwhelmed. Ask yourself: *What's the one thing I could do differently moving forward?* Then review your inclusive leadership action plan based on this additional information.

- Adapting working schedules is the top reasonable accommodation for disabled employees. You'll find the inclusive leadership habits related to work-life integration in the chapter "Supporting work-life integration."

Remember all the great things that disability inclusion can bring you: greater engagement, greater productivity, and a better understanding of your customer's needs, amongst others. The effort to make progress is well worth it.

Practice

Once you're clear on the habits you want to integrate into your life, start practicing them. When they become second nature to you, review your commitments, add new habits, and keep going. Inclusive leadership is a journey, not a destination.

Twelve inclusive leadership habits to promote disability inclusion

Fairness – Are you being fair?

- **Identify and challenge biases about disabled people**

  Challenge common myths about disabled people such as "Disabled people are less productive, are difficult to accommodate, are less reliable, etc." Challenge negative team reactions, particularly if you're about to welcome a new team member with a visible disability or a current team member returning to work after an illness or an accident.

- **Make sure your disabled team members can progress as much as others**

  Being given fewer responsibilities and fewer promotions are the top two issues for disabled people already employed. Verify that this is not happening in your team.

Empathy – Are you treating others as they'd like to be treated?

- **Ask all candidates if they need any adjustments during the hiring process**

  As you never know which candidate might have a specific need, make this a standard question to everyone. But make sure you don't ask questions about a person's health or disability condition, as this is unlawful. Be explicit about the job tasks and working environment, and ask the person how she or he would perform her/his mission. Focus on the person's abilities, not on his or her disabilities.

- **Talk regularly with disabled employees about their accommodation needs**

  The individuals themselves know what works best for them. Do this during the induction period and when people return to work after sick leave. Then monitor regularly if everything is OK. Don't forget to ensure accessibility to the canteen, toilet, printer area, and other common facilities.

- **Get closer to employees whose attendance, behaviour or performance changes**

  Be attentive to changes that might reveal that an employee is experiencing a health problem. Ask how you could help and what additional support they need. Get closer to employees on long-term sick leave to find out how they are doing; show your support.

- **Carefully prepare the return of employees coming back from long sick leaves**

  Make them feel welcome, find out from them what support they need, do all you can to accommodate them. If that's not possible, look proactively for reassignment opportunities within your organisation.

- **Use inclusive language**

  A good rule of thumb is to avoid words that carry a negative connotation and expressions that define people in terms of their disability. For example, say "Disabled people" or "People with disabilities" rather than "The disabled"; say "She has dyslexia" rather than "She's dyslexic"; say "He has a heart condition" rather than "He suffers from a heart condition"; say "A person who's not disabled" rather than "A normal person". If you don't know how to refer to a person's condition, ask her or him.

- **Respect confidentiality**

  You should keep an employee's disability status confidential unless the employee has made it clear they are happy for the information to be shared. This is particularly relevant regarding invisible disabilities. Disabled employees might feel embarrassed and concerned about the reaction of others.

- **Educate yourself about specific disabilities in your team**

  It's impossible to summarise here what behaviours are most appropriate for all different types of disabilities. But the internet is full of resources. A good general tip is to humbly ask people what their main difficulties are, and what you need to do to support them.

Proactivity – Are you accelerating positive change?

- **Send your job ads to organisations specialised on disability inclusion**

  This massively increases your chances of getting qualified, disabled candidates. You can also consider contacting associations that support disabled students for internship positions or temporary workers agencies with proactive disability policies. Make it clear on your job ads that you'll provide adjustments during the recruitment process and on the job if needed.

- **Pair disabled new hires with a mentors**

  Studies show that disabled people with a mentor have a much more positive workplace experience and higher satisfaction with their career progress than those without a mentor.[134] Mentors also have an opportunity to understand better what it's like to have a disability.

- **Raise your team's awareness about disabilities**

  Share with your team your key learnings from this chapter. Prepare your team for the arrival or return of a person with a disability (with the person's consent and guidance), particularly if it's a severe or visible type of disability. This will increase your chances of successfully (re)integrating a person with a disability in your team.

  You can take advantage of different disability dates throughout the year (European or national disability week; international day of people with autism, with depression, etc.) to organise awareness raising events. An easy way to do this is to find, in your organisation, disabled people willing to come and share their experiences with your team. But be careful not to reinforce stereotypes. I've been in an organisation that had organised "wheelchair tours" in the office to raise awareness about accessibility. The intent was positive. But the activity only reinforced the association: disabled people = people on wheelchairs.

The Inclusive Leadership Propeller Model ©

Twelve inclusive leadership habits to promote disability inclusion

Fairness – Are you being fair?

- Identify and challenge biases about disabled people
- Make sure your disabled team members can progress

Empathy – Are you treating others as they'd like to be treated?

- Ask all candidates if they need any adjustments during the hiring process
- Talk regularly with disabled employees about their accommodation needs
- Get closer to employees whose attendance, behaviour or performance changes
- Carefully prepare the return of employees coming back from long sick leaves
- Use inclusive language
- Respect confidentiality
- Educate yourself about specific disabilities in your team

Proactivity – Are you accelerating positive change?

- Send your job ads to organisations specialised on disability issues
- Pair new hires with a disability with a mentor
- Raise your team's awareness about disabilities

9

NAVIGATING CROSS-CULTURAL DIFFERENCES

"All people are the same; only their habits differ."
—Confucius

Delicacy in France

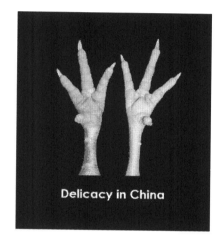

Delicacy in China

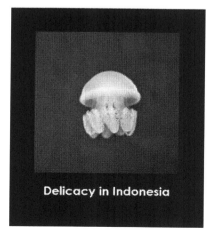

Delicacy in Indonesia

Delicacy in Mexico

With globalisation, increased migrant flows, and technology progress, multicultural teams are increasingly commonplace[1]

Cross-cultural research and training have existed for many years. But up until recently, they were mostly focused on expats. With globalisation, increased migrant flows, and technology progress, more and more leaders lead multicultural teams. Even if they've never left their home countries.

I recently spoke with the director of a growing start-up who felt the need to become more cultural savvy as he manages a virtual global team with employees based in Europe, Asia, and the US. A survey found that 64 percent of multinational employees are involved in virtual teamwork, with many team members based in different countries.[135] In big cities, it is not uncommon to work in a multi-cultural environment, with colleagues born all over the world.

One of my biggest drivers in life has always been to live and work internationally. I'm fascinated by different cultures and languages. I married a foreigner. And international assignments are by far more exciting to me than "domestic" ones. I belong to this increasing species of "global cosmopolitans," people with extensive international experience and a positive attitude towards cultural differences. Even global cosmopolitans can struggle at times to feel comfortable with and not to be judgmental of other cultures. I had an American boss whose emails were so short, with no niceties at all, that they felt like a stab in my heart.

This chapter equips you with the knowledge and tips to avoid cultural misunderstandings and navigate nimbly cultural differences.[136]

---

[1] Cross-cultural diversity is closely linked to ethnic and religious diversity. I strongly recommend you read the chapters "Embracing ethnic diversity" and "Creating a faith-friendly environment."

WHAT YOU NEED TO KNOW

Key concepts

- Culture is defined as "the ideas, customs, and social behaviour of a particular people or society."[137] Culture describes group behaviours, not individual behaviours. Individuals are unique and are influenced by different group cultures (national, corporate, professional, family cultures, etc.). So, don't be surprised when you meet a Russian who doesn't behave in the typical "Russian way."

- Often when we refer to cross-cultural differences in the workplace, we are referring to different national cultures. However, the paradigm "country equals culture" is changing with immigrant flows. In fact, research shows that there can be more cultural gaps within countries than between countries.[138] For instance, a group of mathematicians from different countries might share more in common than a random group of people from the same country.

- Ethnic diversity versus cross-cultural diversity. There are overlaps between the two concepts. But ethnic diversity refers mostly to the cultural diversity you can find within a country (nationals and immigrants), whereas cross-cultural diversity refers mostly to different national cultures.

Six key barriers for cross-cultural management

- **Ethnocentrism**

  We all have a natural tendency to look at other cultures through our own lenses. Ethnocentrism happens when we implicitly believe our way of doing things and seeing things is the right and only way. As a result, we negatively judge behaviours that don't conform to our world vision. We perceive other's behaviours as odd and improper. Ethnocentrism also creates an "us versus them" mentality that can be detrimental. In a previous company I worked for, countless times

I've heard the French complain about the Americans in an ethnocentric way and vice-versa.

- **Stereotyping**

  It's also common to rely on oversimplified clichés about people from different cultures. In fact, there are quite a few cross-cultural trainings in the market that are focused on memorizing cultural differences and can reinforce stereotyping. Learning about differences can be useful as a starting point. But individuals are unique; you can never predict a person's behaviour based on his or her nationality. When we were moving to the UK, French friends told us, *The British never invite you for dinner*, which is a common social activity in France. We happen to have the loveliest British neighbours who invite us for dinner often.

- **Psychological barriers**

  To manage cross-cultural teams successfully, you need to flex your own style. It's not easy to go against your natural preferences. People can feel unauthentic and incompetent. I know the case of a French manager who went to the United States. He found out that his typical French style of giving feedback, focused on what was "wrong" rather than on what was working well, was undermining his team's confidence. He realised what the problem was, but he felt artificial acting the "American" way. He went back to France as soon as he could.

- **Language barriers**

  All teams have a common language, but when some people are more fluent than others, it creates social distance between members. In global teams, people who are less fluent in English tend to withdraw from communication, which means the team may not get all the input it needs. Understanding what's said can be challenging if people speak too fast or use too much slang. This also might have an influence on how people's competence and performance are perceived. I worked for an organisation where non-English native speakers felt that their career progression opportunities were not the same as for English native speakers.

- **Geographical distance**

  In global virtual teams, people don't get the chance to interact and build relationships with each other as in a traditional office environment. And the less you know about people, the less you share information with them. Collaboration within virtual teams is, therefore, more challenging. Groups outside of the head office can also feel excluded. On the other hand, head office group members might think that other colleagues are not contributing. Differences in time zones also can be challenging. Often if you're not in the headquarters, you are expected to cope with meeting timings that are less convenient. I know of a highly talented woman who left a global senior leadership role because she got tired of having frequent meetings in the night.

- **Conflicting values**

  Culture is like an iceberg: what you see are the behaviours, and those are influenced by the invisible values under the water line. Cultural clashes happen when other people's behaviour compromises our own values. Often, when you don't understand or don't agree with a behaviour, it means that there are conflicting values under the water line. There is no right or wrong way of doing things; it's just a matter of cultural norms. Below, you'll see a (non-exhaustive) list of common conflicting cultural values:

  ✓ **Task oriented vs. relationship oriented**

  In some countries like the US, people view conversations as an opportunity to exchange information. People get down to business quickly. In Latin American countries, for instance, conversations are primarily an opportunity to enhance the relationship. I once worked for an American company where, in meetings, participants barely introduced each other; we got down to work immediately. Being a Latin American, it took me a while to get used to it.

✓ **Direct vs. indirect communication**

In countries like Germany, it is a sign of professionalism to speak clearly and leave no room for misinterpretation. In countries like Korea, people prefer to communicate indirectly. People approach problems through vague references. The danger here is that a person from a direct culture may come across as insensitive, while the person from the indirect culture may appear imprecise.

✓ **Open vs. subtle disagreement**

Cultures that place a high value on "face" and group harmony may be averse to confrontation, like in China. In other cultures, having a "good fight" is a sign of trust, like in the Netherlands. People from different parts of the world also vary in the amount of emotion they show during professional conversations. For example, Italians raise their voices, while the British are more composed.

✓ **Informality vs. formality**

In some countries, such as Australia, people are generally casual; in others, like Japan, people tend to be more formal. To informal people, formality might be interpreted as the sign of stiffness, while informality to formal people might be perceived as a lack of professionalism.

✓ **Structured vs. flexible scheduling**

All businesses follow timetables, but in some cultures, people strictly adhere to the schedule, whereas in others, they treat it as a suggestion. For some, "five minutes" could mean half an hour, and "tomorrow" could mean the next few days. In Brazil, I wouldn't start a meeting exactly on time. It feels disrespectful not to wait a bit for the late comers. In the UK, not starting the meeting on time might be considered disrespectful towards those who made it to the meeting on time.

✓ **Egalitarian vs. hierarchical**

Team members from more egalitarian countries, such as Sweden, may be accustomed to voicing their unfiltered opinions and ideas, while those from more hierarchical cultures tend to speak up only after more senior colleagues have expressed their views. I ran quite a few audits in Morocco, and people's behaviours were totally different, depending on whether their bosses were in the same room or not.

WHAT YOU NEED TO DO

Reflect

- Do you have people from different nationalities in your team?
- Are you good at engaging people from different countries?
- Are you judgmental when you come across different cultural behaviours?
- Do you feel comfortable flexing your style to adapt to different cultural preferences?
- Do people from different nationalities have the same chances to enter and progress in your team?
- How would your team members answer these questions about you?
- Would people from different nationalities have similar views?

If, upon reflection, you think you're doing well, CONGRATULATIONS! If you feel there's a lot of room for improvement, no problem. Either way, the Inclusive Leadership Propeller Model © will help you improve your ability to navigate cross-cultural differences.

Commit

Find below the specific inclusive leadership habits applied to cross-cultural management:

- Don't take them in isolation. They reinforce and complement the inclusive leadership basic habits you've seen in PART I of this book.
- Don't get overwhelmed. Ask yourself: *What's the one thing I could do differently moving forward?* Then review your inclusive leader action plan based on this additional information.
- Cross-cultural diversity is closely linked to ethnic and religious diversity. I strongly recommend you read the chapters "Embracing ethnic diversity" and "Creating a faith-friendly environment."

Remember all the great things that cross-cultural management can bring you: greater engagement, greater productivity, and a better understanding of your customer's needs, amongst others. The effort to change is well worth it.

Practice

Once you're clear on the habits you want to integrate into your life, start practicing them. When they become second nature to you, review your commitments, add new habits, and keep going. Inclusive leadership is a journey, not a destination.

Twelve inclusive leadership habits to navigate cross-cultural differences

Fairness – Are you being fair?

- **Don't stereotype individuals based on their nationality**
  Individuals are unique; you can never predict a person's behaviour based on his or her nationality. Besides, nobody likes to be treated like a cultural stereotype.

- **Give everyone a chance to contribute**

  In all teams, there's a risk that the more extrovert colleagues monopolise the discussions. This risk grows in cross-cultural teams because some cultures are more vocal than others and some people might be more fluent speakers than others. Here are some tactics you can use: go around the table (or conference line/video chat screens) at least once so that everyone has a chance to speak; circle back to the quiet people after a meeting; ask people to jot down ideas anonymously before you open the debate.

- **Monitor assignments, evaluations, and promotions by nationality**

  This will help you prevent biases towards those who are based in headquarters, are more fluent in English or are closer to you culturally.

Empathy – Are you treating others as they'd like to be treated?

- **Educate yourself about cross-cultural differences and similarities**

  This can help you avoid cultural faux pas, make sense of other's behaviours, and create connections at the same time. You can do this through researching but also by asking expats and most importantly, by asking people themselves about their own culture. You can say, "This is how I give feedback in my culture; how does it work in yours?" Asking questions is a good icebreaker. People like to talk about their own cultures, and with the talking comes understanding and connection. Use this information only as a starting point, and be open to deviations from the norm. Be mindful of differences but don't obsess over them. Sometimes culture matters; sometimes it doesn't.

- **Find out the rationale behind unfamiliar behaviours to you**

  When a behaviour doesn't make sense to you, avoid being judgmental. For the people behaving in that way, there's certainly a rationale. It's up to you; find it out. Figure out which underlying values are causing a problem (see the most common value conflicts above). And ask people. State the facts, tell your story, and ask for the other person's version. Remember my boss whose super concise emails hurt my feelings? He simply didn't want to waste my time, out of respect for me.

- **Flex your style**

  Just knowing about a difference conceptually is not enough. You need to practice new behaviours in real situations. For example, being more directive with a team that doesn't feel comfortable with a more participate leadership style, delivering more positive feedback in a culture that values encouragement. Play with adaptations; see how people react.

- **Speak plainly and not too fast**

  So that everyone can understand you, especially during virtual meetings. But please don't slow down too much as you may sound patronising. My husband had a Parisian friend who used to speak very slowly with me. Her intentions were positive; she was mindful of the fact that French wasn't my first language. But she made me feel a bit stupid. Sadly, it's better to avoid jokes, slang, or cultural references that might be confusing to a non-native speaker. I just facilitated a workshop on cross-cultural management, and for a few participants, the recurrent jokes that they couldn't fully understand made them feel excluded. Recapping key points orally and in writing at the end of meetings can also be helpful.

- **Respect different time-zones**

  Try to find meeting times that are respectful of everyone's work life integration, rotate meeting time if that's not possible. Also, respect local holidays and people's vacation time. This sounds so basic, yet many people are invited to participate in meetings during a bank holiday for them. They either participate in it or miss a meeting where important decisions might have been taken. In some countries, people are not entitled or expected to take a lot of vacation; in others, taking three weeks off in a row is common.

Proactivity – Are you accelerating positive change?

- **Raise your team's cultural awareness**

  Share with your team what you've learned in this chapter, encourage intercultural mentoring, use national holidays to trigger cultural conversations. For instance, during a team meeting close to Chinese New Year, you could ask a Chinese team member to explain to others what it means and how he/she celebrates it. Some team members might need to be coached by you to understand their colleagues' behaviours and to adapt to different cultural expectations.

- **Build your team's emotional bonds**

  When people know each other better, they trust each other more, they collaborate more. That's why trust is the single most important characteristic of a high-functioning team. And when people trust each other in cross-cultural teams, cultural differences don't matter as much. Organise social activities, schedule time for unstructured social chats at the end or at the beginning of meetings; ask for people to give a virtual tour of their offices, to share their bio's; connect team members who you know have things in common (two astronomy lovers, for instance).

- **Invest in languages**

  Encourage your team members who struggle to speak the common language (usually English) to improve their language skills. You can also learn a few words (hello, thank you, goodbye) in the languages of your team members; they will feel valued. I do this whenever I go to a foreign country. I can tell you it does make a difference in the way people relate to you.

The Inclusive Leadership Propeller Model ©

Twelve inclusive leadership habits
to navigate cross-cultural differences

Fairness – Are you being fair?

- Don't stereotype individuals based on their nationality
- Give everyone a chance to contribute
- Monitor assignments, evaluations, and promotions by nationality

Empathy – Are you treating others as they'd like to be treated?

- Educate yourself about cross-cultural differences and similarities
- Find out the rationale behind unfamiliar behaviours to you
- Flex your style
- Speak plainly and not too fast
- Respect different time-zones

Proactivity – Are you accelerating positive change?

- Raise your team's cultural awareness
- Build your team's emotional bonds
- Invest in languages

10

EMBRACING ETHNIC DIVERSITY

"Instead of being colour blind, we need to be colour brave."
—Mellody Hobson

Ursula Burns
Chairman of
Xerox Corporation

Rakesh Kapoor
CEO of RB

Tidjane Thiam
Chief Executive of Crédit Suisse

Soumia Malinbaum
Head of business development
of Keyrus

Ethnic diversity is a recurrent theme in the political scene[2]

Out of all inclusion and diversity topics, ethnic or racial diversity is the one that gets the most media attention. Immigration is a recurrent theme in the political scene across Western countries, particularly in times of economic downturn. In 2016, "Xenophobia" was named Word of the Year by Dictionary.com.[139]

I'm writing this chapter a few months after Trump's election and the Brexit vote. Anti-immigration speech played a key role in both political events. And in both cases, they unchained a wave of hate crimes against ethnic minorities. In the UK, for instance, the number of hate incidents rose by 58 percent in the week following the vote to leave the European Union.[140]

Ethnic diversity is also the most historically loaded inclusion and diversity topic, given our collective experiences with colonialism, slavery or the holocaust. It's about racism, and nobody is comfortable talking about racism.

Race is the very first thing our unconscious minds capture when we meet strangers, yet we don't even know which words to use to talk about it in the workplace. How do you engage the conversation about a person's cultural heritage without being offensive?

Nobody knows what will happen politically in the years to come. But even if countries were to close their borders, the marketplace and the workplace will continue to be more and more ethnically diverse. That's why the ability to discuss race will become increasingly vital to being a leader.

This chapter equips you with the right knowledge and tools to succeed in building and engaging an ethnically diverse team, without alienating the ethnic majority.

---

[2] Ethnic diversity is closely linked to cross-cultural and religious diversity. I strongly recommend you read the chapters "Navigating cross-cultural differences" and "Creating a faith-friendly environment."

WHAT YOU NEED TO KNOW

Key concepts

- **Race or Ethnicity?**

  Race is mostly a biological concept. From a scientific point of view, there's only one human race. However, in many countries, such as the US, the term race is used referring to a person's physical characteristics, such as traits, skin, hair, or eye colour. Ethnicity is rather a sociological concept. It refers to cultural factors, including nationality, regional culture, ancestry, religion or language. This term is more popular in Europe. Some countries, such as France, prefer to avoid the terms race or ethnicity and refer to diversity of origins or people with immigrant backgrounds. I'm personally more comfortable with the term ethnicity.

- **Ethnic and racial minorities vary across countries**

  What unfortunately doesn't vary is the fact that wherever you go in the world, some populations will be the target of racist discrimination. It might be people born in the country or immigrants. Jews are a traditional ethnic minority in many countries (I chose to talk about Jews in the religious diversity chapter, though). Romanis are the biggest and most discriminated ethnic minority in Europe. In the US, we're talking mostly about African Americans and Hispanic and Latino Americans. In France, it is mostly about Arabs and Black people. In the UK, it's Asians and Black minorities. You can also have racism against people from a certain region or with a certain accent, as it's the case in Brazil (people from the North East) and Italy (people from the South). Discrimination can also happen towards indigenous people, such as the Inuits in Canada, the Aborigines in Australia, or native Americans in the US. In Africa, race discrimination can happen between different ethnic groups.

- **Racism**

  Racism is the belief that people's qualities are influenced by their race and that the members of other races are not as good as the members of your own.[141] Racism can be overt or subtle. You can have an unconscious racial bias without consciously being racist. I was shocked the first time I took an implicit bias association test on ethnicity. This free online test developed by Harvard[142] allows you to measure your unconscious bias on different categories. I found out I had a slight bias against Arabs. I was shocked not only because of my values but also because my mother-in-law, an extraordinary woman who I love dearly, is Arab. I then reflected and realised that, yes, I tended to make the implicit association: Arab men = sexist men. This was a wake-up call for me.

- **Ethnic diversity versus social diversity**

  In many countries, there's a partial overlap between socially disadvantaged populations and ethnically diverse populations. Typically, in France, many companies started tackling ethnic diversity by supporting youth from underprivileged areas. That said, there are many ethnic minority people who are not underprivileged, and who face barriers. This is the focus of this chapter.

- **Ethnic diversity versus cross-cultural diversity**

  There are overlaps between the two concepts. But ethnic diversity refers mostly to the cultural diversity you can find within a country (nationals and immigrants), whereas cross-cultural diversity refers mostly to different national cultures.

Three key facts about ethnic diversity

- **Societies are more and more multicultural**

  The proportion of migrants as a share of the national population in high-income countries rose from nine percent to thirteen percent from 2000 to 2015. Today, minorities makeup 37 percent of the United States population and will climb to 57 percent by 2060.[143]

Thirteen percent of UK's working age population and twenty percent of young people in primary and secondary school are from ethnic minorities.[144] There are usually more babies born in ethnic minority families, so even if we stopped migration today, ethnic minority groups, will continue to grow.

- **Racial discrimination is pervasive**

  For instance, a study carried out in the UK showed that to get a call back for an interview, applicants with ethnic minority sounding names must send nearly two times more applications than applicants with white sounding names with the same qualifications.[145] In France, a study showed that applicants with Arabic sounding names receive three times less callbacks than applicants with identical CVs and typically French sounding names. The gap doubles for management positions.[146] In Austria, a study showed that people with typical Austrian names are invited to job interviews twice as much as people with Nigerian names with the same level of qualification.[147] Similar studies in other countries show similar results. That's what some researchers call the "ethnic penalty."

- **Ethnic minorities are under-represented in management and leadership positions**

  For instance, one in eight British is from ethnic minorities, yet only one in sixteen hold management positions.[148]

Four key myths about ethnic diversity

- **Immigrants are less qualified**

  Immigrants tend to be underemployed. For instance, in the US, immigrants with university degrees from their native countries often work as cab drivers, cleaners or security guards.[149] While only sixteen percent of EU migrants come to England with no qualifications, as many as 42 percent have low-skilled jobs.[150] Insufficient language skills only partially explains this situation.

- **Young people are less racial biased**

  The compiled results of Harvard's Implicit Association Test showed that, contrary to public belief, young people show more racial bias than any other age group.[151] A study in France showed that ethnic bias in young people is just as strong as in people from other age bands.[152]

- **Ethnic minority people are not biased**

  The compiled results of Harvard's Implicit Association Test showed that even if whites are more biased than non-whites (72 percent vs. 60 percent), most people have racial bias.[153]

- **Some industries don't need to improve ethnic diversity**

  Some industries that employ low qualified labour, such as the construction industry, tend to have a higher concentration of people from ethnic minorities. However, when you look closely, you'll find an "ethnic division" of labour, with a hierarchy of jobs that can be done by certain ethnicities, and little social mobility, with very few people from ethnic minorities at management positions. Ethnic diversity across the board is extremely rare. I was once in a factory in Belgium; when I asked the local leadership team if they were diverse, they proudly told me that sixty percent of the factory were immigrants. When I asked which jobs they had, I found out that there was not a single immigrant occupying a management position.

Seven key barriers for ethnic diversity

- **Racial bias**

  Racial bias is pervasive in most societies. For instance, the compiled results of Harvard's Implicit Association Test showed that around seventy percent of Europeans, Americans, and Britons have a racial bias.[154] In Australia, 33 percent of workers are opposed to increased levels of ethnic diversity in their workplace.[155]

116

- ## Discomfort to talk about race and ethnicity

  Talking about race is perceived as divisive and as discriminatory. That's why many people say they are "colourblind." The problem with being "colourblind"—aside from the fact that we're not really—is that it is really a white privilege to be able to ignore race.[156] If you're from an ethnic minority, you know there's a difference in treatment. I have a friend who's the chief editor of a major economic journal in France. He told me that when there's a police control in the underground, he's often controlled. He's black. The discomfort is also worsened by the fact that there's a lack of consensus about the terminology to use, even amongst ethnic minorities. A French study showed that the more you associate a group with negative stereotypes, the more taboo it becomes to name that group. For instance, it's OK to talk about Asians but more problematic to talk about Arabs.[157] In the UK, a recent report was released referring to "people of colour," provoking quite negative reactions from experts. Yet, daring to start the conversations and talk about the "elephant in the room" is what most business leaders and experts recommend nowadays.[158] It's the intent behind the words that matter. In a company I worked for, employees didn't know how to engage in conversations with colleagues from ethnic minorities. Learning that a good conversation starter was *What's your cultural heritage?* (as opposed to *Where do you come from?*) made a big difference.

- ## White resentment

  Many white people, especially if they are unhappy with their status, tend to see ethnic diversity initiatives as an unfair advantage and preferential treatment. Some talk about "reverse racism or discrimination." A 2011 survey found that the average white American believes they face more racial bias than African Americans.[159] There seems to be a denial of white privilege, coupled with a lack of awareness about the real barriers faced by ethnic minorities. As the Nigerian author Chimamanda Ngozi Adichie puts it, however bad your economic situation is as a white person in the US, if you were black, it'd be even worse.[160] This is coupled with a misunderstanding of what inclusion means, i.e., removing the biases that prevent us from focusing on talent, rather than forgetting about talent to focus on people's ethnicity. That's why it's important to make it clear that ethnic diversity is about having a mix of all ethnicities, not only people from ethnic minorities. In the same way that gender balance is about having both men and women in a team, and not only women.

- **Difficulties in measuring and monitoring**

In the business world, it's difficult to manage what you cannot measure. For different cultural and historical reasons, it's legally difficult, if not impossible, to measure people's ethnicity in the workplace in most countries. The US and the UK are exceptions. And even in such countries, the data is not used as it should be. I've worked with an American organisation that kept diversity data completely secret to avoid litigation, even from senior leaders. I've also worked with British companies that didn't make an effort to collect and analyse the ethnic data available.

- **Narrow recruitment pools**

Many companies tend to recruit only from elite universities and business schools. They fail to tap into institutions whose students have a much broader ethnic and social background. In addition, we tend to choose candidates whose degrees and professional experiences we are familiar with. Thus, we overlook foreign candidates with credentials and qualifications from other countries.

- **Self-censorship amongst ethnic minorities**

It's very hard not to internalise the negative stereotypes that the society and the media disseminate about people from ethnic minorities. The lack of positive role models also influences one's belief in succeeding. Thus, many people from ethnic minorities give up before even trying. They say to themselves, *This is not for me; I'll never make it*, and they also hear from others surrounding them, *This is not for you*. My husband's friend, a Martinican living in the suburbs of Paris, was discouraged by most of his teachers to pursue his studies. Fortunately, he met a tutor who believed in him, and this changed the course of his life.

- **Lack of influential contacts amongst ethnic minorities**
People from ethnic minorities tend to know fewer people with the influence to hire or to promote, or with the knowledge about the hiring and promotion opportunities. That's why so many proactive organisations provide ethnic minority employees or ethnic minority students with mentors that can broaden their network of contacts.

WHAT YOU NEED TO DO

Reflect

- Does your team reflect the ethnic diversity of society and of your customers at different hierarchical levels?
- Do people from different ethnicities have the same chances to enter and to progress in your team?
- Are you good at engaging people with different ethnic backgrounds?
- Are you comfortable challenging racist behaviours?
- How would your team members answer these questions about you?
- Would people from different ethnicities have similar views?

If, upon reflection, you think you're doing well, CONGRATULATIONS! If you feel there's a lot of room for improvement, no problem. Either way, the Inclusive Leadership Propeller Model © will help you improve your ability to embrace ethnic diversity.

Commit

Find below the specific inclusive leadership habits applied to ethnic diversity:

- Don't take them in isolation. They reinforce and complement the inclusive leadership basic habits you've seen in PART I of this book.

- Don't get overwhelmed. Ask yourself: *What's the one thing I could do differently moving forward?* Then review your inclusive leadership action plan based on this additional information.

- Ethnic diversity is closely linked to cross-cultural and religious diversity. I strongly recommend you read the chapters "Navigating cross-cultural differences" and "Creating a faith-friendly environment."

Remember all the great things that embracing ethnic diversity can bring you: greater engagement, greater productivity, and a better understanding of your customer's needs, amongst others. The effort to make progress is well worth it.

Practice

Once you're clear on the habits you want to integrate into your life, start practicing them. When they become second nature to you, review your commitments, add new habits, and keep going. Inclusive leadership is a journey, not a destination.

Nine inclusive leadership habits to embrace ethnic diversity

Fairness – Are you being fair?

- **Identify and challenge ethnic bias**

  If you realise people are hesitant to hire or promote someone because of his or her ethnic background, dare to bring the issue to the table. You can take a Harvard Implicit Association[161] test on ethnicity, which is a free online resource, to find out your own biases and suggest your team take it too.

- **Respond when you see disrepecful behaviours and remarks**

  Fight disrespectful behaviours, also when they affect "majority" groups. Don't forget to show your support directly to whoever is the target of such behaviours. I once visited a company where white British employees felt ostracised by Eastern Europeans workers who tended to speak in their own language without realising the negative impact on other colleagues.

- **Post job ads as much as possible**

  Based on the affinity bias principle, if you don't post your job ads, you'll tend to attract more of the people who already belong to your organisation. If your team or organisation is not ethnically diverse, the less reliant you are on word of mouth and referrals, the bigger your chances to attract qualified candidates with diverse ethnic backgrounds.

- **Look at history and data per ethnicity**

  How often have you hired and/or promoted people from ethnic minorities? In which hierarchical levels of your organisation, can you find people from ethnic minorities? Even in countries where ethnic statistics are not available, you can empirically tell where disparities are. I've seen construction sites with a high concentration of ethnic minorities at entry level positions and not a single manager from an ethnic minority. If you're based in a country where ethnic statistics are available (US or UK, for instance), ask your human resources teams to have access to the data so that you can check if your team reflect the ethnic diversity of your labour market and if ethnic minority employees have equal access to promotion and training.

Empathy – Are you treating others as they'd like to be treated?

- **Inform yourself about how ethnicity influences people's experiences**

  You can ask people simple questions like "Do you think ethnicity/race/origin impacts the way people are treated or their chances of getting hired and promoted here?" Get everyone's opinion, including but not only, the opinions of people from ethnic minorities. You'll be able to better understand specific challenges if any, and figure out ways to overcome them.

- **Offer language support to foreign candidates and employees**

  If fluently speaking the local language is not a requirement for the job, helping candidates to fill in forms or giving then more time to perform tasks at the selection stage will increase your chances of identifying qualified foreign candidates. Offering language lessons can also increase the growth opportunities of employees who have the technical skills but not the language skills. I've seen a construction company that offered French lessons to help internal candidates qualify for supervisory roles.

Proactivity – Are you accelerating positive change?

- **Be open to credentials and degrees from non-elite and foreign universities**

  This will broaden your talent pool and increase your chances to reach out to qualified candidates with more ethnic and socially diverse backgrounds. If you're looking for interns, you can also send adds to these organisations.

- **Communicate about your openness to ethnic diversity**

  Tell your human resources, recruitment, and temporary agencies you want to increase ethnic diversity in your team. In this way, you encourage them to consider qualified candidates they might have overlooked, and even to look for candidates in different places. As always, final decisions should always be based on skills and competence.

- **Mentor and sponsor people from ethnic minorities**
Research shows that the one single characteristic that all ethnic minorities who advance in their careers share is a strong network of mentors and sponsors. You can support existing employees, as well as students who are not yet part of the corporate world. You can do this informally or participate in official mentoring programs if your company has any. You can also pair new hires from ethnic minorities with buddies or mentors during the onboarding process.

The Inclusive Leadership Propeller Model ©

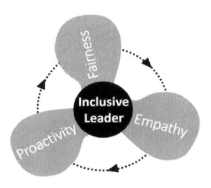

Nine inclusive leadership habits to embrace ethnic diversity

Fairness – Are you being fair?

- Identify and challenge ethnic bias
- Respond when you see disrepectful behaviours and remarks
- Post job ads as much as possible
- Look at history and data per ethnicity

Empathy – Are you treating others as they'd like to be treated?

- Inform yourself about how ethnicity influences people's experiences
- Offer language support to foreign candidates and employees

Proactivity – Are you accelerating change?

- Be open to credentials and degrees from non-elite and foreign universities
- Communicate about your openness to ethnic diversity
- Mentor and sponsor people from ethnic minorities

11

CREATING A FAITH-FRIENDLY ENVIRONMENT

"I wish there was a religion that would not let people either
hate or hurt each other."

—George Sand

Ginella Massa
First hijab-wearing television
news reporter in Canada

Jatinderpal Singh Bhullar
First Buckingham Palace Guard to
wear a Sikh turban

Bal Bansal
Associate Director
IT Innovation & Digital
Coca-Cola European Partners

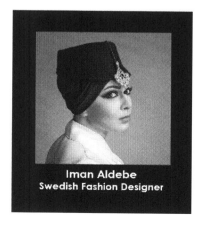

Iman Aldebe
Swedish Fashion Designer

Societies are increasingly multicultural, and with different cultures come different religious[3]

Three trends make religious diversity an important topic for business leaders today:

- Societies are increasingly multicultural, and with different cultures come different religions.

- More and more people want to bring their full selves to the workplace. To many, particularly members of ethnic minorities, their faith and their religious practice are important aspects of their identity.

- At the same time, religious intolerance is on the rise. For instance, fear of persecution affects Jews across Europe, with 23% of Jews surveyed in eight European countries stating that they avoided Jewish events or sites because they feared for their safety.[162]

Religion is a historically sensitive topic, as many wars and tragedies related to religion have taken place in the past. The uneasiness that religious diversity brings can be particularly strong in countries with a secular tradition, such as France, where public religious displays may encounter disapproval by the general population. I recently attended a conference in Paris about religion in the workplace. Most speakers opened their presentations saying that religious diversity was an asset. However, most of them spoke about religious practices as a risk to be managed.

Although this is a theme with many legal implications, I'm focusing on the knowledge and leadership behaviours, beyond minimum legal requirements, that will empower you to attract and engage people of all faiths, including people with no faith.

---

[3] Religious diversity is closely linked to cross-cultural and ethnic diversity. I strongly recommend you read the chapters "Navigating cross-cultural differences" and "Embracing ethnic diversity".

WHAT YOU NEED TO KNOW

Key concepts

- **Freedom of religion**

  Freedom of religion is the fundamental human right to believe or not in religion. The right not to be discriminated on religious grounds is also a universal human right. But there's an important distinction between the right to believe and the right to practice a religion. The right to believe is absolute: you're totally free to believe or not in whatever belief system you want. The right to practice religion in the workplace can be limited under certain circumstances (see below).

- **Indirect discrimination**

  This concept is particularly relevant regarding religious diversity, although it applies to all types of diversity. It happens when a practice that applies to everyone disadvantages people of a certain religion. For example: by introducing a uniform which does not permit head coverings, you would be indirectly discriminating female Muslims wearing a hijab or Sikhs wearing a turban.

- **Reasonable accommodations**

  In many countries, employers are required to accommodate religious practices of employees, unless doing so creates an undue hardship for employers. As an inclusive leader, you should try to accommodate employee's religious needs as much as possible. What's reasonable will vary, depending on the country where you are and the employee's role. But there's a simple framework you can use in most cases. Asking yourself the following questions can help you determine whether an accommodation is reasonable:

1. Does it negatively affect the employee's ability to do their job? Wearing a hijab usually doesn't affect a person's ability to do their job.
2. Does it negatively impact the business? That would be the case if too many people asked to take a day off on the same day for religious reasons, leaving customers unattended.
3. Does it compromise health, safety or security? In France and Canada, for instance, in construction worksites, everybody is requested to wear a hard hat for safety reasons, including Sikhs.
4. Does it disadvantage other employees or customers? If an employee wants to pray during his break time in a quiet room, this usually doesn't disadvantage anyone.
5. Does it breach equality laws? That would be the case if an employee refused to obey a female manager for religious reasons, or if an employee refused to work with a gay co-worker for religious reasons.
6. Does it infringe the freedom of belief of other employees? A friend of mine told me that in her team, in Brazil, evangelical employees would tune to the evangelical radio station every lunch break. She politely asked those wishing to listen to that radio station to wear head phones, out of respect for those who weren't evangelical. She had a good reflex.

When you're considering a religious practice, ask yourself the questions above. If your answer is "no" to these questions, there's no reason why you shouldn't accommodate an employee's religious practice. To be on the safe side, always double check with your human resources team.

Three key facts about religious diversity

- **Religious hostility is on the rise**
  For instance, in the US, the number of charges related to religious discrimination rose by fifty percent between 2005 and 2015.[163] In the UK, between 2014 and 2015, there was a 43 percent increase in

religion-related hate crimes.[164] The 2015 Eurobarometer on discrimination notes an increase in anti-Semitism and Islamophobia in Europe.[165]

- **Most religious requests are easily accommodated**

  For instance, in France, in 85 percent of cases, religious requests are easily managed.

- **Taking time off for religious reasons is the most popular request**

  For instance, in Belgium (21 percent of accommodations) and France (forty percent of accommodations), this is the top type of accommodation reported by companies.[166]

Five key barriers to building a faith-friendly environment

- **Religious bias**

  Fifty percent of Europeans (76 percent of French and 48 percent of British) believe religious discrimination is widespread. One in eight Europeans (thirteen percent) say they would be uncomfortable working with a Muslim person. This is higher than for any of the other religious groups.[167]

- **Judgmental attitude**

  Religion can be a delicate topic, as some people have strong views about it. In the workplace, some people tend to judge others' behaviours according to their own personal values. If they agree with a practice, they will accommodate it; if they think it doesn't make sense, they will reject it. This is not a good attitude. As an inclusive leader, you should analyse religious practices objectively (see framework above), independently of your personal views.

- **Lack of guiding principles**

  Many managers facing religious requests feel lost. They tend to either accommodate all practices for fear of discriminating, even when such practices disadvantage other employees and the business. Or they reject all accommodations in order to treat everybody the same, without realising the negative impact on those who have specific religious needs. Sometimes managers discriminate employees and candidates on behalf of their clients or their employees, believing that's a valid reason, when it's not. A few years ago, a Moroccan colleague of mine told me that as she was looking for a job, recruiters would tell her that although she was a good fit for the job, their clients wouldn't appreciate dealing with a woman wearing a veil.

- **Assumptions about religious practices**

  Often managers don't know much about other religions or tend to make assumptions. During a manufacturing site visit in the UK, I met a Sikh team leader who told me his manager had created a prayer room for him, believing Sikhs needed to pray like Muslims when it's not the case. Also, not everyone who holds a religion follows the same practices and may differ considerably in their level of observance. For instance, not all Muslims practice Ramadan, not all Jews practice Sabbath, not all Christians rest on Sundays.

- **Misconceptions about secularism**

  In countries like France, secularism is an important value. It means that the State has no religion and it guarantees the freedom of religion for everyone. Thus, civil servants, as State representatives, are required to be neutral, i.e., not to display any visible religious signs. This doesn't apply to employees of private companies. However, many people believe that visible religious displays are not allowed in companies, or even in public spaces, which is incorrect.

WHAT YOU NEED TO DO

Reflect

- Do you have people from different religions in your team that you're aware of?

- Do you feel comfortable accommodating different religious practices?
- Do people from different religions have the same chances to enter and to progress in your team? Are you good at engaging people of various religions?
- How would your team members answer these questions about you?
- Would people from different religions have similar views?

If, upon reflection, you think you're doing well, CONGRATULATIONS! If you feel there's a lot of room for improvement, no problem. Either way, the Inclusive Leadership Propeller Model © will help you improve your ability to create a faith-friendly environment.

Commit

Find below the specific inclusive leadership habits applied religious diversity:

- Don't take them in isolation. They reinforce and complement the inclusive leadership basic habits you've seen in PART I of this book.
- Don't get overwhelmed. Ask yourself: *What's the one thing I could do differently moving forward?* Then review your inclusive leadership action plan based on this additional information.
- Religious diversity is closely linked to cross-cultural and ethnic diversity. I strongly recommend you read the chapters "Navigating cross-cultural differences" and "Embracing ethnic diversity".

Remember all the great things that creating a faith-friendly environment can bring you: greater engagement, greater productivity, and a better understanding of your customer's needs, amongst others. The effort to make progress is well worth it.

Practice

Once you're clear on the habits you want to integrate into your life, start practicing them. When they become second nature to you, review your commitments, add new habits, and keep going. Inclusive leadership is a journey, not a destination.

Nine inclusive leadership habits to create a faith-friendly environment

Fairness – Are you being fair?

- **Identify and challenge religious biases**

  We're prone to biases especially regarding people who display visible signs of religious practice, such as a veil or a kippah. A good question to bring objectivity to this emotional topic is, "How does his or her religion impact his/her the ability to do the job?" It usually doesn't.

- **Use a structured process to assess religious requests**

  You've seen above a set of six questions to use whenever a team member has a religious accommodation request. They will help you to stay away from personal considerations about people's religious practices and treat everyone consistently.

Empathy – Are you treating others as they'd like to be treated?

- **Be open to accommodating employees' religious practices**

  In a normal work day (9 a.m. to 5 p.m.), Muslims who pray generally pray twice—at lunch time (1 p.m.) and late afternoon (4 p.m.). If people wish to use their break time to pray, be flexible. Praying doesn't take longer than smoking. If possible, let people know that they can use a quiet room to pray. This could be an empty meeting room, for instance. You don't have to do this. But why not doing it if a quiet place is available and allowing its use for prayer doesn't disrupt the business or others? But make sure you don't assign a room to a specific religion. Quiet rooms should be for people practicing all religions. In Sweden, I've seen a factory whose employee engagement and productivity rates went up once the site director created a prayer room. On Fridays, Jews might want to leave earlier for the Sabbath. If it's feasible, for the business and the team, they might work extra time another day to make up for it. Talk with staff about fasting during Ramadan. Discuss if it's helpful to hold meetings in the morning or early afternoon or to let staff finish earlier if a lunch break is not taken.

- **Consider holidays requests for religious reasons just like any other request**

  Which means accepting a request if it doesn't negatively impact the business needs or other team members. Anticipating holidays as much as possible is good practice anyway, even if you only have atheists in your team.

- **Check religious festivals calendar when planning events and meetings**

  Don't schedule events on important religious dates. You don't have to take everything into account, but at least the main religious holy days such as The Holy week (Christians), Diwali (Hindus), Passover (Jews), Eid al-Fitr (Muslims). I've seen a company organising the annual leadership convention during Passover, which made Jewish directors feel excluded. I just came back from a training where a practicing catholic finance director complained about a major company event being organised during the Holy week.

- **Consider dietary restrictions**

  If you're organising a meal, ask if people have any dietary restrictions (no need to refer to religion here). This is good practice anyway, as many people are veggies, vegans or have food allergies nowadays. If you can't ask, provide a variety of food. You don't have to provide Halal or Kosher, but if you do, make sure there are also options for those who don't eat Halal and Kosher. If alcohol is served, make sure that non-alcoholic drinks are also available. When arranging work-related social gatherings, bear in mind that not all employees feel comfortable going to places where alcohol is served, such as pubs and bars. You can vary the places you go together as a team.

- **Be mindful of people's modesty values**

  For religious reasons, some people might want to avoid eye or skin contact with people from the opposite sex, cover themselves (veil), or they may want to avoid certain types of clothing (too tight or too short). Be flexible, but at the same time, make sure that others in the team don't feel discriminated against. For instance, if a man doesn't want to shake hands with women, depending on your country culture, you might want to advise him to avoid shaking hands with everyone, to ensure equality.

Proactivity – Are you accelerating positive change?

- **Raise your team's awareness about religious diversity**

  Share with your team members what you learned in this chapter. During important religious festivities, ask team members who are comfortable doing it to explain what it means to them and how they practice it. I had once an Indian colleague who explained to the team, during a routine team meeting, what Diwali meant to her and how she was celebrating it. Another Israeli team member shared with the team the recipes she cooked during Sabbath. Everybody appreciated it, and the colleagues who were sharing their traditions felt valued.

- **Use religious events to strengthen relations within the team**

  In some organisations, to avoid discrimination, people stopped celebrating everything, including Christmas. I don't think this is a positive approach. Celebrate things together as a team every time it's possible. I've seen Muslims bringing to the workplace pastries to celebrate with non-Muslim colleagues the end of Ramadan, and everybody was thrilled. I've seen leaders wishing Happy Diwali to

12

FOSTERING AN LGBT-INCLUSIVE CULTURE

"If a bullet should enter my brain, let that bullet destroy every closet door."
—Harvey Milk

Alain Joyce
CEO of Quantas Airlines
Openly gay

Inga Beale
CEO of Lloyds of London
Openly bisexual

Gigi Chao
Hong Kong Business women
Openly lesbian

India Willoughby
TV Presenter
Transgender

LGBT Inclusion is the litmus test for how truly inclusive an organisation is

LGBT[4] (lesbian, gay, bisexual, transsexual) inclusion is one of the most taboo inclusion and diversity topics. It's also been described as the litmus test for how truly inclusive an organisation is of all types of diversity.[168]

There are strong views in our societies regarding sexuality and religious belief systems that disapprove of homosexuality. This means that you can be at risk if you are, or are perceived as, an LGBT person.

Often when I make presentations or facilitate trainings on this subject, I can sense people's discomfort in their giggling or in their explicit objections, such as "Why talk about your sex life at work? It's nobody's business." Some are even afraid I might ask them what their sexual orientation is. People confuse sexual orientation and sex life and think LGBT inclusion is about counting the number of LGBT people.

For LGBT people, an inclusive culture allows them to relax, be authentic and fully engage at work. Your key objective as an inclusive leader is to create a safe space where, regardless of whether someone is out or not, they are assured that it wouldn't be an issue if they were. Here's what you need to know and do to create an LGBT-friendly culture.

---

[4] The LGBT term is evolving. Some say LGBTI, where the I refers to intersexual people. Others add the letter Q referring to "queer", which would be considered a less appropriate term in the UK. For simplicity sake, I'll refer to LGBT in this chapter.

WHAT YOU NEED TO KNOW

Three key LGBT facts

- **The number of LGBT people**

  The estimated number of people who identify as lesbian, gay or bisexual is between six to ten percent. The estimated number of transsexual or transgender people is 0.3 percent of the population. [169]

- **The number of LGBT people who come out**

  Only a minority of people come out. In the UK, for instance, only 33 percent of gay men, 23 percent of lesbians, and 12 percent of bisexual people are out at work. [170]

- **The number of suicidal attempts amongst LGBT people**

  The number of suicidal attempts is staggering high for LGBT people compared with the overall population. For instance, 4.6 percent of the overall US population has self-reported a suicide attempt. This number climbs to 20 percent for lesbian, gay or bisexual respondents, and up to 41 percent for transgender respondents. [171]

One key myth about LGBT

- **You can tell by the look of a person whether he or she is LGBT**

  Only eight percent of the lesbian and gay population fit the majority stereotype of what a lesbian or gay person looks or acts like. [172] A man can be feminine without being gay; a woman can be masculine without being lesbian. Transsexual and intersexual individuals can also have ambiguous looks.

Five key obstacles for LGBT inclusion

- **Hostile legislation**

  Legislation towards homosexuality is evolving positively in some geographies, with many countries adopting protective laws of LGBT people, including same-sex marriage in fifteen countries (mostly Western countries). However, there are countries that don't prohibit discrimination against LGBT people (China and Turkey, for instance), 75 countries that criminalise same-sex sexual conduct, and 8 countries where same-sex sexual conduct is punishable by death.[173]

- **Hostile belief systems**

  In a society with diverse cultural, religious and individual values and beliefs, not everyone is supportive of LGBT inclusion. However, LGBT inclusion is not about changing people's personal beliefs. It's about preventing destructive behaviours against LGBT.

- **Hostile behaviours**

  All over the world, LGBT people report unfair treatment. In Australia, for instance, 53 percent of lesbians and gay men experience harassment and discrimination and 50 percent experience homophobic remarks/jokes in the workplace. In the UK, 88 percent of transgender employees experience discrimination or harassment at work.[174]

- **Lack of awareness about heterosexual privilege**

  We are humans, not robots. In the workplace, we feel the need to build report, to connect on a personal level and to have healthy social conversations. Most heterosexuals don't realise that their sexual orientation is on display most of the time when they do trivial things such as: talking freely about their families, about their partners, about what they did during the weekend, bringing their partners to social events, displaying their photos on their desks. I often ask people to experiment not displaying anything about their personal lives in the office for a month to see how it feels not to bring your full self to work.

- **The closet burden**

  Given all hostility towards LGBT people, many LGBT prefer not to "come out of the closet." Research has found that LGBT "in the closet" can be as much as twenty percent less productive because of the effort that it takes daily to constantly self-edit, avoid questions, and not give too much away.[175] On the bright side, LGBT people who do come out are around seventy percent more likely to be satisfied with their managers.[176] I met a senior leader who explained to me how hard it was for him to decide whether to come out or not whenever he met a new person, including clients. Because he never knew what the reaction was going to be. He found it exhausting.

WHAT YOU NEED TO DO

Reflect

- Do you have LGBT people in your team who have come out?
- Does the fact that someone is LGBT, or is perceived as an LGBT, impact his or her chances to enter or to progress in your team?
- Is there a chance that an LGBT person might not feel safe coming out in your team?
- Are you comfortable challenging gay jokes in the workplace?
- How would your team members answer these questions about you?
- Would LGBT and non-LGBT people have similar views?

If, upon reflection, you think you're doing well, CONGRATULATIONS! If you feel there's a lot of room for improvement, no problem. Either way, the Inclusive Leadership Propeller Model © will help you improve your ability to foster an LGBT-inclusive culture.

Commit

Find below the specific inclusive leadership habits applied to LGBT inclusion:

- Don't take them in isolation. They reinforce and complement the basic inclusive leadership habits you've seen in PART I of this book.
- Don't get overwhelmed. Ask yourself: *What's the one thing I could do differently moving forward?* Then review your inclusive leadership action plan based on this additional information.

Remember all the great things that fostering an LGBT-friendly culture can bring you: greater engagement, productivity, and retention, amongst others. The effort to make progress is well worth it.

Practice

Once you're clear on the habits you want to integrate into your life, start practicing them. When they become second nature to you, review your commitments, add new habits, and keep going. Inclusive leadership is a journey, not a destination.

Nine inclusive leadership habits to foster an LGBT- inclusive culture

Fairness – Are you being fair?

- **Identify and challenge bias against LGBT people**

  For instance, respond when you hear people speculating about someone's sexual orientation or gender identity. Especially when such speculation is related to a decision to hire or to promote someone.

- **Respond when you see homophobic or transphobic jokes and behaviours**

  One of the most quoted reasons for not coming out at work is the fear to become the target of banter. A manager once told me that she didn't see the harm in cracking gay jokes if nobody around was gay. I asked her, "Would you find it OK to crack jokes about black people if nobody in the team is black? And, how can you tell nobody in your team is gay or has close relatives and friends who are gay?" Transphobic behaviours are widespread. For example, make sure nobody prevents a transsexual employee to use the toilets or changing rooms of his/her expressed gender identity.

Empathy – Are you treating others as they'd like to be treated?

- **Respect people's privacy**

  Don't ask people about their sexual orientation or gender identity history. Don't disclose to others what someone may have disclosed to you. Disclosing is a highly private and sensitive topic. LGBT inclusion is not about forcing people to come out or finding out who is LGBT. It's about creating the space where people feel comfortable to do so if they want.

- **Use inclusive language such as partner rather than husband/wife**

  Don't assume everybody's heterosexual. Always assume there are LGBT people in your team or organisation. I once met a Canadian executive who had received an invitation to participate in his company's annual leadership convention. He felt excluded because the invitation was clearly addressed to him and his wife when, in fact, he had a male partner. Also, use the pronoun transsexual colleagues prefer when referring to them. If you don't know what to say, ask them whether they prefer to be referred to as "he" or "she" and respect their choice.

- ,**Inform yourself about how it feels to be an LGBTperson at work (if you're not one)**

  Openly talk to LGBT colleagues, friends or family members about their challenges and situations in the workplace that made them feel included and excluded. You'll be able to better understand and support LGBT team members.

- **Learn about your company's LGBT policies and benefits**

  So that you can communicate about them to your team, support transgender employees transitioning, and LGBT team members assigned to work in countries hostile to LGBT people.

Proactivity – Are you accelerating positive change?

- **Show visible support to LGBT inclusion**

  Just as you cannot tell a person is LGBT unless he or she tells you, an LGBT person cannot guess which would be your level of support to them unless you make it clear. You can show your support in different ways. I once met a gay leader who made a point of talking openly about his same-sex partner every time it was appropriate. He had realised how important it was for people to see visible senior role models. Another director would talk about his daughter's same-sex family to make people feel comfortable. You can also use visible signs such as rainbow email signatures, a rainbow cup, or a rainbow sticker in your office (check if it's OK with your organisation beforehand).

- **Raise your team's awareness about LGBT inclusion**

  Share with them your key learnings from this chapter. Have someone from your LGBT network present to your team. Explain to employees uncomfortable with the topic that LGBT inclusion is not about forcing anyone to change their views; it's about ensuring everyone is treated with respect. Use dates such as the international day against homophobia and transphobia, or gay pride dates, to engage in conversations around the topic with your team members.

- **Participate in your company's LGBT network**

  Activities may include networking events, mentoring programs, training for LGBT and allies. You can also encourage participation by your team members. If your company doesn't have a network, consider creating one.

The Inclusive Leadership Propeller Model ©

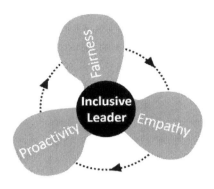

Nine inclusive leadership habits
to foster an LGBT-inclusive culture

Fairness – Are you being fair?

- Practice identifying and challenging bias against LGBT people
- Respond when you see homophobic or transphobic jokes and behaviours

Empathy – Are you treating others as they'd like to be treated?

- Respect people's privacy
- Use inclusive language such as partner rather than husband/wife
- Inform yourself about how it feels to be an LGBT person at work (if you're not one)
- Learn about your company's LGBT policies and benefits

Proactivity – Are you accelerating positive change?

- Show visible support to LGBT inclusion
- Raise your team's awareness about LGBT inclusion
- Participate in your company's LGBT network

13

SUPPORTING WORK-LIFE INTEGRATION

"I don't believe we have a professional self Monday through
Friday and a real self the rest of the time. It is all
professional, and it is all personal."
—Sheryl Sandberg

Katie McQuaid
Director at Amazon
Part-timer

John Duncanson
Managing Director Capgemini Scotland
Part-timer

Simon Allport
Managing Partner EY
Part-timer

Natalie Lyons
Director at Société Générale
Part-timer

Everybody wants a better work-life integration for different reasons at different life stages

Everybody needs more time because we all have more pressure to perform with fewer resources and more information to process. And we're constantly connected.

Although people grasp the connection between gender diversity and work-life integration, not everyone sees the strong connection between work-life integration and most inclusion and diversity topics. When I run inclusion and diversity focus groups, as soon as I start asking people questions about work-life integration, some people seem surprised and happy at the same time. Although they didn't expect to talk about it, they have a lot to say. That's particularly true for white heterosexual males who don't identify with other inclusion and diversity themes.

Work-life integration is an inclusion topic because it's about adapting to people's different needs and preferences, often by giving them more flexibility, and ultimately the choice regarding where, when, and how to work.

Improving work-life integration has a ripple effect on many other inclusion and diversity dimensions. It has a huge impact on your ability to attract, develop and retain the growing number of female workers, young and divorced parents, the "sandwich generation" (those caring for children and ageing parents), people who want to practice their religion, who have an active social or community life, people who want to work flexibly towards retirement and disabled people needing flexibility in their work schedule.

Yet, we're often afraid. To give more flexibility and to ask for it. We fear to step into uncharted territory. Because for flexibility to work, you need trust between manager and employee, clarity about expectations, and a smart way to measure performance. If these are missing, flexibility can be a double-edged sword, creating challenges for individuals and the organisation.

In this chapter, I give you the keys to supporting different ways of working for a better work-life integration amongst your team members, including those who want to work more conventionally.

WHAT YOU NEED TO KNOW

Key concepts

- **Work-life integration or work-life balance?**

  "Work-life balance" implies that there are clear boundaries between work and life, that these are two separate and competing things. It also implies that to be happy, you need to find the balance between both. "Work-life integration" seems to me an adequate term nowadays. We bring more of our personal lives to work and more of our work to our personal lives. Life and work are complementary to each other, with success in one aspect contributing to success in the other. The focus shifts from balancing things to better combining different aspects of life into an integral whole.

  I have personally struggled a long time to find "work-life balance." Then one day, I had a liberating conversation with a Belgium senior leader who I admired profoundly. She seemed to always have time. She told me, "I don't have a work and a life. My work is part of my life. I don't have to balance things that are not opposed to each other." That conversation made me see things in a different way. I felt relieved of the pressure to achieve a "balance" that is almost impossible to reach or to keep all the time.

- **Flexible working – what are the options?**

  Flexible working is one of the main ways to promote work-life integration, although not the only one. It describes any type of working arrangement that gives some degree of flexibility on how long, where, and when employees work. It can be formal or informal, permanent or temporary. Not all forms of flexible working are suitable for all types of work, but a degree of flexibility is possible for most jobs. For instance, I often hear that manufacturing jobs are not suitable to flexible working. It's not true. I've known a Swedish site director who used to arrive very early and leave the site around 3 p.m. to pick up her children. I've seen line workers choosing their shifts and working part time.

The most common forms of flexible working are:

- Part-time working – you work less than full-time hours.
- Job sharing – a form of part-time where you split a job between two people.
- Compressed hours – you work usual hours in fewer days, for instance, you work four long days, instead of five normal days.
- Home working, telecommuting or teleworking – you take work to do at home.
- Flexitime – there's a core time (for example, from 10 a.m. to 3 p.m.), with flexible start (for example, from 7 a.m. to 10 a.m.) and finish (for example, from 3 p .m. to 7 p.m) times. This allows people to start or finish their days earlier or later.

Three key facts about work-life integration

- **Managing work-life is becoming more difficult**
  - ✓ A global survey showed that one in three workers say managing work-life has become more difficult, with four in ten managers saying that their hours have increased over the past five years.[177]
  - ✓ Three out of four employees say they don't have enough time.[178]
  - ✓ 98 percent of executives check email during their off time, and 63 percent check email every one to two hours during their off time.[179]

- **Work-life integration is important for employees**
  - ✓ One in three workers cites flexible working as the most important employer attribute.[180]
  - ✓ Half of the employees report that they would choose a flexible working arrangement over a pay rise, and almost a third indicated that they would look to change employers if flexible work was offered elsewhere.[181]
  - ✓ Having a boss who doesn't allow you to work flexibly is one of the top five reasons for quitting a job.[182] That was one of the reasons why I personally changed jobs at some point.
- **Flexible working is beneficial for employers**
  - ✓ **Employee satisfaction**

    A total of 47 percent of people who have the option to telework are "very satisfied" with their jobs, compared to 27 percent of those who are office bound.[183]
  - ✓ **Productivity**

    Over two-thirds of employers report increased productivity among their teleworkers. Contributing factors include fewer interruptions from colleagues, more effective time management, feelings of empowerment, and longer hours.[184] British Telecom proved that productivity of flexible workers increased by thirty percent.[185]
  - ✓ **Decreased absenteeism**

    In a study, one-third of companies saw a decrease in absenteeism after they implemented flex-time policies.[186] Another study showed a reduction in absenteeism from twelve percent to two percent amongst those that worked flexibly.[187]
  - ✓ **Savings**

    A study found that halftime home based work accounts for savings of more than $10,000 per employee per year. Such savings are the result of increased productivity, reduced facility costs, lowered absenteeism, and reduced turnover.[188] A manufacturing company I worked for used part-time work to accommodate employees near retirement. Absenteeism rates dropped among those who chose to work part time. In addition, as they started volunteering more to work overtime, the site made considerable savings by paying less to temporary agencies.

Five key barriers for work-life integration

- ### Lack of management support

  Managers have many questions when they are confronted with flexibility requests. Typically: "How will I know if she is really working?"; "How will I manage his performance?"; "How will I adapt his workload to his part time?"; "What if everybody asks the same?"; "What if this negatively impacts the business?"; "What if this puts an extra burden on other team members?"; "What if home workers feel isolated?" These are all valid questions, and to handle them, you need some guidance that's often missing in organisations. Keep reading to find out more about it in the "what you need to do" section.

- ### The flexibility stigma

  Often people fear that working flexibly or taking time off will have a negative impact on their careers. This happens even when people are entitled to take time off or when they work for companies that have robust work-life integration policies in place. A global EY survey showed that one in ten people have suffered a negative consequence for working flexibly. Negative consequences included losing a job, being denied a promotion or raise, being assigned to less interesting or high-profile assignments or being publicly or privately reprimanded.[189]

  The flexibility stigma is even stronger for men, because of the traditional stereotypes about gender roles that see men as breadwinners and women as carers. Working fathers are twice as likely as working mothers to have flexible working requests turned down.[190] The stigma affects even the most senior leaders. I once met the CEO of a leading British parking company who told me a "secret": since he'd got divorced, he'd decided to work four days a week to look after his three children. The only person aware of it in the company was his personal assistant. He wasn't sure how his employees would have reacted.

- **The presentism culture**

  The presentism culture rewards attendance over output. Lack of trust and the inability to measure performance objectively favour such culture. In such environments, employees may stay late or arrive early, just to impress their bosses and colleagues. I've seen a company where when people left at 5 p.m., they'd hear from their boss, "Are you taking the day off?"

- **The 24/7 culture**

  With increased connectivity comes a risk of never switching off. People feel more and more the often-implicit pressure to check and to respond to emails at any time. I once audited a Swedish company whose numbers of burn-out cases were increasing exponentially. Interestingly, their engagement scores were very high. People felt so committed to the company that they were overworking until the point of no return. One of the biggest problems pointed out by employees interviewed was the fact that they got messages from their colleagues and managers all the time and felt the need to respond to them immediately. The 24/7 expectation tends to be higher for senior leaders, especially if you're leading global teams across different time zones.

- **Lack of senior role models**

  Having senior leaders who are in dual-career families, who work flexibly and who have a sustainable lifestyle is not common. Having senior leaders on part-time is rare. That's why I chose to feature a few part-time leaders at the beginning of this chapter. And that's also one of the reasons why so many women stop projecting themselves in more senior roles. There seems to be only one way to be a respectable leader, and that's working all the time. I once worked for a company where all executive committee members were married, had big families (three to six children), and stay-at-home wives. They were the traditional breadwinners who seem to devote all their time to work. Flexible working wasn't a priority for them. I've also met a managing director whose family was living in another city. He stayed at work until very late because he didn't feel like going back to an empty home. His behaviour had a very negative impact on his employees, who felt that they had to stay late, particularly since the most strategic conversations were happening after normal office hours, around a beer.

WHAT YOU NEED TO DO

Reflect

- Do you work flexibly?
- Do you encourage flexible working?
- Do you have team members working flexibly?
- Do people working flexibly have the same chances as others to enter and to progress in your team?
- Is working 24/7 something you expect from your team members?
- Do you need to see people in the office to believe they are working?
- How would your team members answer these questions about you?
- Would people working flexibly and people working conventionally have similar views?

If, upon reflection, you think you're doing well, CONGRATULATIONS! If you feel there's a lot of room for improvement, no problem. Either way, the Inclusive Leadership

Propeller Model © will help you improve your ability to support work-life integration.

Commit

Find below the specific inclusive leadership habits applied to work-life integration:

- Don't take them in isolation. They reinforce and complement the basic inclusive leadership habits you've seen in PART I of this book.
- Don't get overwhelmed. Ask yourself: *What's the one thing I could do differently moving forward?* Then review your inclusive leadership action plan based on this additional information.

Remember all the great things that work-life integration can bring you: increased employee satisfaction, productivity, and retention, amongst others. The effort to make progress is well worth it.

Practice

Once you're clear on the habits you want to integrate into your life, start practicing them. When they become second nature to you, review your commitments, add new habits, and keep going. Inclusive leadership is a journey, not a destination.

Eleven inclusive leadership habits to support work-life integration

Fairness – Are you being fair?

- **Identify and challenge biases against people working flexibly**

  These include thoughts and remarks such as "He took a year off; he's not very ambitious"; "She's on part-time; she's not committed to her career"; or "He leaves early often; he's not taking his job really seriously." A dear friend of mine, who is also a senior leader, told me he once overlooked an excellent candidate for a sales position only because the candidate had taken a sabbatical year, which didn't convey a "professional" attitude to him at the time.

- **Treat flexibility requests from men and women in the same way**

  It doesn't' matter why people are asking to work flexibly. What matters is whether their request is feasible or not, based on the impact on the service, the team, and the business. The exceptions are the cases where you're legally required to accommodate people's requests, for example, for disabled employees or working parents. Check with your human resources team as these vary in different countries. In the UK, for instance, employees are entitled to make a flexible work request, that can only be rejected if there's a sound business reason for it. [191]

- **Adapt the workload to people on part-time**

  Often people working part-time are paid less and keep the same workload, which is not fair. I've seen this happening even in the Netherlands, the country with the highest share of part-timers in the world. At the same time, make sure that the rest of the team doesn't have an additional workload when someone goes on part-time. See how the work can be done differently.

- **Look at history and data with a flexible working lens.**

  Ask yourself "Are people working flexibly being penalised when it comes to performance reviews, pay raises or promotion opportunities?" On one occasion I was having a conversation with a director who suddenly realised that in her company, she had never seen somebody working part time getting a promotion.

Empathy – Are you treating others as they'd like to be treated?

- **Ask your team members, individually, what could be done to improve their work-life integration, and together, work on feasible solutions**

  You can do this during annual reviews if you notice team members struggling for any personal reason (a birth, a death or an illness in the family, a divorce, etc.), or anytime. Little costless tweaks might make a big difference for some employees during certain periods of their lives. For instance, arriving and leaving the office earlier or working from home one afternoon per week. I've seen a very interesting case of an employee who couldn't switch off. His manager spoke with him and coached him so that he could work smarter, not harder.

- **Agree with your team on guidelines for meetings and email communications**

  Guidelines could include: not starting meetings too early in the morning, or too late in the day; not sending emails during the weekends or on holidays, avoiding last minute requests, etc. I've seen a director who loved sending emails on Saturday mornings to his direct reports without realising that this was causing stress in his team. He then started using the delayed delivery option, and that made a big difference to everyone. Another senior leader decided to avoid meetings on Thursdays and Fridays so that the team could have quality time to work on projects. Get creative and see what works best for your team. I have added to the end of my emails "My emails sent in the evenings and during the week-ends do not require an immediate reply".

- **Check in with remote and home workers regularly**

  One of the risks of working from home or remotely is the isolation feeling and lack of guidance. Regularly review achievements, give feedback, and ask questions about how people feel and what you could do to help. Also, make sure they have the tools and technology they need, and know how to prioritise tasks.

Proactivity – Are you accelerating positive change?

- **Be a good role model**

  Leaders who have a good work-life integration give permission to employees to do the same. Talk about your family life, your hobbies, bring your full self to work. Tell your employees if you're working from home. I've met a CEO who loved running marathons and encouraged his employees to take time off to do sports. I recently saw an inspiring post on Linkedin: a letter from Joe Biden, Barak Obama's Vice President, to his team members encouraging them to prioritise family events in their lives.

- **Advertise roles as open to flexible working**

  And make sure you mention it to the candidates you're interviewing. Some time ago, I was being interviewed for a position, and one of the key reasons that made me say yes to the job offer was the fact that the hiring manager told me he was open to flexible working. So, I happily left a manager who made me feel guilty every time I worked from home to work with a manager who empowered me to do my job my way.

- **Get better at evaluating performance**

  In this way, you and your employees will become much more comfortable about flexible working. Evaluating performance well means not relying on a generalised impression of people's work, but agreeing on clear and measurable goals.

- **Run a flexible working pilot**

  This is a smart way to introduce flexible working in a team or in an organisation that's not used to it. Give it a try, and decide what to do next based on the results of the experiment on the teams' performance, wellbeing, and engagement.

The Inclusive Leadership Propeller Model ©

Eleven inclusive leadership habits
to support work-life integration

Fairness – Are you being fair?

- Identify and challenge biases against people working flexibly
- Treat flexibility requests from men and women in the same way
- Adapt the workload to people on part-time
- Look at history and data with a flexible working lens

Empathy – Are you treating others as they'd like to be treated?

- Ask your team members, individually, what could be done to improve their work-life integration, and together, work on feasible solutions

- Agree with your team on guidelines for meetings and email communications

- Check in with remote and home workers regularly

Proactivity – Are you accelerating positive change?

- Be a good role model
- Advertise roles as open to flexible working
- Get better at evaluating performance
- Run a flexible working pilot

CONCLUSION

"People will forget what you said, people will forget what you did, but people will never forget how you made them feel."

—Maya Angelou

Adopt the inclusive leadership mindset

I hope by now you are confident to be an inclusive leader. You found out what it means to be an inclusive leader, why it matters, and how to make it happen. You learned:

- The inclusion and exclusion mechanisms that are common across all types of differences.
- The inclusive leadership skills and habits you need to develop in different leadership situations.
- The specific barriers and inclusive leadership habits related to different inclusion and diversity dimensions: gender, generations, disability, nationality, ethnicity, religion, sexual orientation, and work-life integration.

Most importantly, you can adopt the inclusive leadership mindset using a framework, the Inclusive Leadership Propeller Model © and its mantra—*How fair, empathetic, and proactive am I?*—that you can apply to navigate all sorts of human differences. Including those we didn't cover in this book, such as differences in personality types, in thinking, learning, and communication styles.

You certainly noticed the recurrence in the chapters. I hope you didn't mind it, because the repetition is to make it easier for you to develop the inclusive leadership mindset. As Zig Ziglar puts it so well, *Repetition is the mother of learning, the father of action, which makes it the architect of all accomplishment.*

Be mindful, focus on talent, and don't forget the majority

Key messages to take away:

- If you're not intentionally including, you might be unintentionally excluding. Inclusive leadership requires you to be mindful of what you do, and the impact you have on others. Particularly at times of stress and change.

- Inclusion is not about hiring or promoting the "diverse person"; it's about removing the barriers, often unconscious, that prevent you from focusing on skills and competence and from recognizing talent when it comes in different sizes and shapes. Never think you have to choose between diversity and quality.

- Inclusive leadership is not about accommodating minorities. It's about adapting to everybody's differences, including those differences that the "majority" brings. After all, we're all different, not from each other, but like each other. Inclusion is not an "us versus them" game. It's a togetherness game where everybody should win.

Take it step by step

Succeeding as an inclusive leader is not a 'quick hit' you can achieve by reading this book alone. It's like running a marathon: it's simple, but it's not easy.[192] It's about your mindset and your behaviours. It requires your willingness to see and to do things in a different way. And your discipline to integrate, gradually, new habits in your life. It takes practice and perseverance to make behaviours automatic. This will be uncomfortable at times, and you'll tend to go back to default mode under pressure. But staying comfortable doesn't make you progress. And the more confident you're to step out of your comfort zone, the more competent you'll become.

You've read about many inclusive habits. You cannot integrate them all at once. You're not a superhuman; nobody is. The single most powerful habit you can adopt to shape your mindset is to think about the inclusive leader mantra as often as possible until it becomes second nature to you: *How fair, empathetic, and proactive am I?* Get started by prioritising the habits that build on your strengths, and that are the most urgent and relevant to you. Reassess yourself regularly with the help of the 30-question self-assessment. And review your action plan by adding one new habit at a time. There'll always be room for improvement.

Focus on your influence zone

This book empowers you to lead inclusively wherever you're, no matter how inclusive or non-inclusive the organisation you work for. Of course, you don't live in isolation; organisations, depending on their policies and strategies, can make it more difficult, or easy, for you to lead inclusively. Focus on what you can control. There's a lot you can do without needing permission or resources of anyone else. Everyone, including individual contributors, has an influence zone. You have the power to influence positively your direct reports, your peers, your hierarchy, and beyond. Your influence comes a bit from what you say, a lot from how you behave, and mostly from how you make people feel.

I discovered that, in the inclusive leadership journey, the most common way people give up their power is by thinking they don't have any. They believe the responsibility and power to change is elsewhere. Employees think inclusion should come from their managers. Managers think it should come from senior leaders. Senior leaders think the human resources teams should be in charge of it. Human resources teams say the responsibility is in the hands of line managers, and so on. Some even say "The problem comes from society, the school system, the media; there's nothing corporations can do." The truth is, there's a responsibility chain. Nobody can make inclusion happen alone, but everyone has a role to play. And you, as an inclusive leader, play a key role in this symphony. And the more power you have, the bigger your opportunity and responsibility to hold others accountable for inclusion. The average baboon looks at the group leader once every twenty to thirty seconds for guidance. Human beings aren't much different.[193]

Dare to make it happen

One of my favourite heroes of all times is Rosa Parks. She was an African American lady who lived in the US during the segregation period. She became a symbol of the civil rights movement by refusing to give up her seat to a white passenger on a bus in 1955. I'm not telling you to become an activist. But what I find very inspirational in her attitude is the impact a single person can have just by being brave enough to do the right thing. What she did was very simple. She didn't give up her seat. Everybody could have done it. But it was not easy. What set Rosa Parks apart was her courage to do it. I hope you, too, have the courage to be inclusive, especially when it involves challenging the status quo. If you're in the majority group, use your privilege to influence change. If you're different from the majority, be a visible role model and inspire others.

Your efforts will pay you great dividends

By becoming an inclusive leader, you'll be able to spot talent more easily. You'll be able to build teams with a greater diversity of thoughts, where everyone, no matter how different they are, can give their best. You'll be able to find ways to motivate and influence different people so that you can achieve your goals more easily. By leading inclusively, you can also find more purpose in your career, because you'll be helping to build a better business in a better world. When you make people count, you count more to people. You leave a more meaningful legacy that you can measure—for example, by imagining what your team members would say about you during your funeral mass. But please, don't get me wrong; I wish you a long and healthy life! And I hope you'll be a positive change agent wherever you go.

Good luck in your inclusive leadership journey!

Congratulations for getting to the end of this book. This already sets you apart from most people and tells me how committed you are. I wish you the best of luck in your inclusive leadership journey!

To encourage you and support you on your journey, I'm offering you free bonuses. Simply go to the following webpage to have instant access to them: **www.declicinternational.com/bookbonuses**

If you enjoyed reading this book and think others would benefit from it, I will be immensily grateful if you can post a review on Amazon. Your feedback is invaluable and will help me share this message with more people. All you have to do, if you are happy to leave a review, is go the review section on this book's Amazon page. Just scroll down to "customer review" and write. Thank you for your feedback and thoughts. This would be a great way to start flexing your inclusive leadership proactive muscles too.

I look forward to hearing from you. Until then, embrace differences and make a difference!

PHOTO CREDITS

CHAPTER 6

Ana Maria Botin

By World Economic Forum from Cologny, Switzerland - Ana P. Botin - World Economic Forum Annual Meeting Davos 2009 Uploaded by Rastrojo (D•ES), CC BY-SA 2.0, https://commons.wikimedia.org/w/index.php?curid=9111413

Justin Trudeau

By Justin Trudeau c/o:Brian Cobbledick (Flickr) [CC BY 2.0 (http://creativecommons.org/licenses/by/2.0)], via Wikimedia Commons

Isabelle Kocher

By Swaf75 - Own work, CC BY-SA 4.0, https://commons.wikimedia.org/w/index.php?curid=48963162

Sheryl Sandberg

By World Economic Forum from Cologny, Switzerland - Women in Economic Decision-making: Sheryl SandbergUploaded by January, CC BY-SA 2.0, https://commons.wikimedia.org/w/index.php?curid=24178494

CHAPTER 7

Malala

By Claude Truong-Ngoc / Wikimedia Commons - cc-by-sa-3.0, CC BY-SA 3.0, https://commons.wikimedia.org/w/index.php?curid=29737649

CHAPTER 8

Abraham Lincoln

CHAPTER 9

CHAPTER 10

CHAPTER 12

REFERENCES

INTRODUCTION

[1] http://www.catalyst.org/media/catalyst-study-reveals-financial-performance-higher-companies-more-women-top.
[2] http://www.mckinsey.com/business-functions/organization/our-insights/why-diversity-matters.
[3] People and Partnership, Confederation of British Industry, December 2016.
[4] SAP Workforce 2020, Oxford Economics, 2014.
[5] Women in the Workplace, Mckinsey & Company and Lean In, 2016.

CHAPTER 2

[6] Kellye Whitney, Business case for diversity: my Foot, May 2016.
[7] Bridget Brennan, Top 10 things everyone should know about women consumers, January 2015.
[8] The Economist Intelligence Unit, Engaging and Integrating a Global Workforce, SHRM Foundation, February 2015.
[9] Eurostat: http://ec.europa.eu/eurostat/statistics-explained/index.php/EU_citizenship_-_statistics_on_cross-border_activities, April 2013.
[10] Kira Hudson Banks, How Managers Can Promote Healthy Discussions About Race, Harvard Business Review, January 2016.
[11] http://www.disabledworld.com/.
[12] EY, Tracking global trends: how six key developments are shaping the business world, 2010.
[13] The world at work, McKinsey Global Institute, 2012.
[14] http://www.mckinsey.com/business-functions/organization/our-insights/why-diversity-matters.
[15] http://www.catalyst.org/media/catalyst-study-reveals-financial-performance-higher-companies-more-women-top.
[16] Sylvan Ann Hewlett, Melinda Marshall & Laura, Sherbin with Tara Gonsalves, Innovation, diversity and market growth, Center for talent Innovation, September 2013.
[17] Out in the world infographics, Center for Talent Innovation, 2016.
[18] https://www.glassdoor.com/press/twothirds-people-diversity-important-deciding-work-glassdoor-survey-2/
[19] Charles Duhig, What Google learned from its quest to build the perfect team, New Yort Times, February 2016.

[20] Korn Ferry survey conducted with more than 400 global executives in August 2013. http://www.kornferry.com/press/15143/

[21] Lucy Ward and John Carvel, Best ideas come from work teams mixing men and women, The Guardian, November 2007.

[22] Hong and Page, Groups of diverse problem solvers can outperform groups of high-ability problem solvers, PNAS, November 2004.

[23] Stephen Frost and Danny Kalman, Inclusive Talent Management, Kogan Page, 2016.

[24] http://www.engagementisnotenough.com/pdfs/Cost_of_Engagement.pdf.

[25] Absentéisme, les DRH tenté par la politique du baton, L'économiste, May 2008.

[26] https://www.americanprogress.org/wp-content/uploads/2012/11/CostofTurnover.pdf.

CHAPTER 3

[27] Senior Management roles held by women, Grant Thornton UK LLP London, March 2016.

[28] https://www.oecd.org/gender/data/genderwagegap.htm.

[29] Bertrand, Marianne and Sendhil Mullainathan, Are Emily And Greg More Employable Than Lakisha And Jamal? A Field Experiment On Labor Market Discrimination, American Economic Review, September 2004.

[30] A snapshot of ageism in the UK and across Europe, Age UK, March 2011.

[31] Annual Review of the Human Rights Situation of Lesbian, Gay, Bisexual, Trans and Intersex People in Europe , IGLA Europe, 2014.

32 Disability statistics - barriers to social integration – Statistics Explained, Eurostat, November 2015.

[33] Baromètre sur la perception des discriminations au travail Janvier, Ifop, 2014.

[34] Roy F. Baumeister and John A. Bargh, Conscious and Unconscious - Toward an Integrative Understanding of Human Mental Life and Action, February 2014.

[35] http://www.psychologicalscience.org/index.php/publications/observer/2006/july-06/how-many-seconds-to-a-first-impression.html.

[36] Mahzarin R. Banaji, Max H. Bazerman and Dolly Chugh, How (Un)ethical Are You? Business Harvard Review, December 2003.

[37] Adam Quinton, The Paradox of Meritocracy - in Tech, May 2016.

[38] Proven strategies for addressing unconscious bias in the workplace, Diversity Best Practises, CDO Insights, August 2008.

[39] Daniel Kahneman, "Thinking, Fast and Slow," Farrar, Straus and Giroux, 2011.

[40] Nilhil Swaminathan, Why Does the Brain Need So Much Power? April 2008.

[41] Lin Bian, Sarah-Jane Leslie, and Andrei Cimpian, Gender stereotypes about intellectual ability emerge early and influence children's interests, Science, January 2017.

[42] Tiffany Pham, Think you're not biased against women at work? Read this, December 2016.

[43] Hinton, Eric L.; Young, Stephen, When Small Slights Lead to Huge Problems in the Workplace, DiversityInc, April 2013.

[44] Shivali Best, Can a computer tell if you're RACIST? Algorithm can detect hidden prejudice from a person's body language, Mail On Line, September 2016.

[45] Adrienne B. Hancock, Influence of communication partner's gender on language, The George Washington University, 2015.

[46] https://en.wikipedia.org/wiki/Mansplaining

[47] Cook Ross, Everyday Bias: further explorations into how the unconscious mind shapes our world at work, 2014.

[48] Tiffany Pham, Think you're not biased against women at work? Read this, December 2016.

[49] Tiffany Pham, Think you're not biased against women at work? Read this, December 2016.

[50] https://implicit.harvard.edu/implicit/takeatest.html.

[51] Adam Quinton, The Paradox of Meritocracy - in Tech, May 2016

[52] I Don't Feel Your Pain: Why We Need More Morality and Less Empathy, Heleo Editors, December 2016.

CHAPTER 4

[53] https://www.theguardian.com/business/2016/oct/25/gender-pay-gap-170-years-to-close-world-economic-forum-equality

[54] Mahzarin R. Banaji, Max H. Bazerman and Dolly Chugh, How (Un)ethical Are You? Business Harvard Review, December 2003.

[55] Stephen Frost and Danny Kalman, Inclusive Talent Management, Kogan Page, 2016.

[56] Stephen Frost and Danny Kalman, Inclusive Talent Management, Kogan Page, 2016.

[57] Charlotte Sweeney, Fleur Bothwick, Inclusive Leadership,Pearson, 2016.

CHAPTER 5

[58] Charles Duhigg, "The Power of Habit", Ramdom House, 2012.

[59] Inspired by the conscious ladder of competence created by Noel Burch in 1970.

CHAPTER 6

[60] https://www.theguardian.com/business/2016/oct/25/gender-pay-gap-170-years-to-close-world-economic-forum-equality

[61] Women matter 2012, Mckinsey Company, 2012.

[62] Johanna Barsh and Lareine Yee, Unloccking the full potential of women at work, McKinsey & Company, 2012.

[63] Women Matter 2012 and Women Matter 2016, McKinsey & Company, 2012.

[64] Women at Work: Trends 2016, International Labour Office, 2016.

[65] Nikki Goodway, Gender pay gap: Male traders get double the bonuses of women, the Independent, March 2016.

66 https://www.entrepreneur.com/article/237224.

[67] Philip Cohen, The problem with mostly male (and mostly female) workplaces, The Atlantic, March 2013.

[68] Koch, Amanda J.; D'Mello, Susan D.; Sackett, Paul R., A meta-analysis of gender stereotypes and bias in experimental simulations of employment decision making, Journal of Applied Psychology, January 2015.

[69] Tips for managers, Lean In, 2016, thttp://leanin.org/tips/managers.

[70] Mums-to-be fear telling the boss: Half of working women are nervous about telling manager they are pregnant, Daily Mail, July 2013.

[71] Jenny Garett, Women pushed out of work after maternity leave, 3 Plus International, February 2017.

[72] Est-il toujours difficile d'annoncer sa grossesse à son patron? Marie-Claire, 2013.

[73] Jamila Rizvi, Why the worst decision for women is the best for men, news.com.au, February 2017.

[74] David G. Smith, W. Brad Johnson, Men Can Improve How They Mentor Women. Here's How, Harvard Business Review, December 2016.

[75] Unpaid Care Work: The missing link in the analysis of gender gaps in labour outcomes, OECD, 2014.

[76] Johanna Barsh and Lareine Yee, Unloccking the full potential of women at work, McKinsey & Company, 2012.

[77] https://www.franceinter.fr/economie/sexisme-au-travail-8-femmes-sur-10-concernees

[78] 10 most common sexist office behaviours revealed, HR Grape Vine, September 2015.

[79] Women Matter 2013: Moving corporate culture, moving boundaries, McKinsey & Company, 2013.

[80] Tips for managers, Lean In, 2016, thttp://leanin.org/tips/managers.

[81] Tips for managers, Lean in, 2016, thttp://leanin.org/tips/managers.

[82] A CEO Guide to gender equality, McKinsey&Company, 2015.

[83] Board governance in the age of shareholder empowerment, PwC, 2016.

[84] Biz Carson, This chart shows why it's so hard to fix the diversity problem in tech, December 2016.

[85] https://www.youtube.com/watch?v=c6Xgbh2E0NM

[86] Women in the Workplace, Mckinsey & Company and Lean In, 2016.

[87] shttp://gender-decoder.katmatfield.com/about.

[88] Johanna Barsh and Lareine Yee, Unloccking the full potential of women at work, McKinsey&Company, 2012.

[89] Gretchen Gavett, Generations United, Harvard Business Review, February 2016.

CHAPTER 7

[90] https//oxforddictionaries.com/

[91] Ageism in Europe, a report from EURAGE (European Research Group on Attitudes to Age) commissioned by Age UK, 2011.

[92] The future of work around the world, workforce 2020, Oxford Economics for SAP, 2014.

[93] Macarena Soto Ferri, Generational differences at work, http://scienceforwork.com/blog/category/hr-myth-busting/, 2016.

[94] Gretchen Gavett, Generations United, Harvard Business Review, February 2016.

[95] The Multi-Generational Workforce, Boston College Center for Work & Family, 2015.

[96] The Future of Jobs and Skills, World Economic Forum, 2016.

[97] http://www.futuristspeaker.com/business-trends/2-billion-jobs-to-disappear-by-2030/

[98] http://www.futuristspeaker.com/business-trends/2-billion-jobs-to-disappear-by-2030/

[99] https://workplacetrends.com/the-2015-workplace-flexibility-study/

[100] Tania Lennon, Managing a multi-generational workforce: the myths vs. the realities, Hay Group, 2015.

[101] Ageism in Europe, a report from EURAGE (European Research Group on Attitudes to Age) commissioned by Age UK, 2011.

[102] http://www.jerpel.fr/spip.php?article20.

[103] Soukey Ndoye, Du contrat de génération au management intergénérationnel, AFMD, Novembre 2015.

[104] Jonathan Collie, Segmentation by age is hurting your business, and not in a subtle way either, November, 2016.

[105] https://www.statista.com/statistics/279777/global-unemployment-rate/.

[106] http://www.economist.com/blogs/economist-explains/2013/05/economist-explains-why-youth-unemployment-so-high.

[107] Elisabeth Giret Bertrand, "Non la vie professionneelle ne s'arrete pas à 50 ans », Harvard Business Review France, August 2016.

[108] Elisabeth Giret Bertrand, "Non la vie professionneelle ne s'arrete pas à 50 ans », Harvard Business Review France, August 2016.

CHAPTER 8

[109] Kate Vernon, Towards Disability Confidence - a resource guide to employers in Hong Kong and Singapore, Community Business, April 2011.
[110] This definition is a simplified version of the World Health Organisation's definition that can be found in this link
http://www.who.int/topics/disabilities/en/
[111] Les stéréotypes sur les personnes handicapées, IMS, April 2011.
[112] Kate Vernon, Towards Disability Confidence - a resource guide to employers in Hong Kong and Singapore, Community Business, April 2011.
[113] Carmen Slatton, Why Not Hiring People with Disabilities is Costing You Money and customers, November, 2016.
[114] Disability in the United Kingdom 2016 facts and figures, Papworth Trust, 2016.
[115] Disability in the United Kingdom 2016 facts and figures, Papworth Trust, 2016.
[116] Disability in the United Kingdom 2016 facts and figures, Papworth Trust, 2016.
[117] Disability statistics - barriers to social integration – Statistics Explained, Eurostat, November 2015.
[118] Disability in the United Kingdom 2016 facts and figures, Papworth Trust, 2016.
[119] Disability in the United Kingdom 2016 facts and figures, Papworth Trust, 2016.
[120] Disability in the United Kingdom 2016 facts and figures, Papworth Trust, 2016.
121 Mathias Lebouf, Quand le Handicap se cache, Le Parisien, November 2016
[122] Les stéréotypes sur les personnes handicapées, IMS, April 2011.
[123] Catherine Brooks, "My disability is not always visible": How to create an inclusive workplace for people of all abilities, December 2016
[124] Disability in the United Kingdom 2016 facts and figures, Papworth Trust, 2016.
[125] Disability in the United Kingdom 2016 facts and figures, Papworth Trust, 2016.
[126] Les stéréotypes sur les personnes handicapées, IMS, April 2011.
[127] Réussir le recrutement d'un collaborateur handicapé, Agefiph, 2010.
[128] Maya Hagege and Elena Mascova, Le handicap intégré à la gestion des ressources humaines, AFMD, June 2016.
[129] Les stéréotypes sur les personnes handicapées, IMS, April 2011.

[130] Employees with a visible disability report greater work satisfaction than those with a non-visible disability, Working mother, October 2016.

[131] http://www.disabledworld.com/disability/statistics/

[132] Les stéréotypes sur les personnes handicapées, IMS, April 2011.

[133] Disability in the United Kingdom 2016 facts and figures, Papworth Trust, 2016.

[134] Kate Vernon, Towards Disability Confidence - a resource guide to employers in Hong Kong and Singapore, Community Business, April 2011.

CHAPTER 9

[135] Engaging and Integrating a Global Workforce, The Economist Intelligence Unit, SHRM Foundation, February 2015.

[136] Andy Molinsky's and Erin Meyer's articles inspired a lot of the thoughts shared in this chapter.

[137] https://en.oxforddictionaries.com/definition/culture.

[138] Bradley Kirkman, Vas Taras, and Piers Steel, Research: The Biggest Culture Gaps Are Within Countries, Not Between Them, Harvard Business Review, May 2016.

CHAPTER 10

[139] Jenna Amatulli, Xenophobia' Is Dictionary.com's Word Of The Year, November 2016

[140] Katie Forster, Home Office figures appear to correlate with previous reports of a rise in post-Brexit hate crime, The Independent, October 2016.

[141] http://dictionary.cambridge.org/dictionary/english/racism.

[142] https://implicit.harvard.edu/implicit/index.jsp.

[143] Kira Hudson Banks, How Managers Can Promote Healthy Discussions About Race, Harvard Business Review, January 2016.

[144] Race at Work 2015, BITC, November 2015.

[145] Barney Thompson, Black and ethnic names have less chance of making shortlist, Financial Times, May 2016.

[146] http://www.algerie-dz.com/forums/archive/index.php/t-34368.html.

[147] Shadow Report 2014-15 on Afrophobia in Europe: Key findings, ENAR, 2016.

[148] Fleur Bothwick, How important is the terminology we use when talking about ethnicity? November 2016.

[149] Ibrahim Hirsi, Why do many highly educated immigrants face underemployment? Minn Post, October 2015.

[150] https://www.euractiv.com/section/socialeuropejobs/

opinion/areeumigrantsoverqualifiedforthejobstheydo/.
[151] http://race.bitc.org.uk/all-resources/infographics.
[152] Les stéréotypes sur les origines, IMS, December 2013.
[153] http://race.bitc.org.uk/all-resources/infographics.
[154] http://race.bitc.org.uk/all-resources/infographics.
[155] Ethnic diversity in the workplace 'tolerated but not embraced', The Australian, November 2016.
[156] John Halstead, The Real Reason White People Say 'All Lives Matter, July 2016.
[157] Baromètre Adia- Observatoire des discriminations Novembre 2006.
[158] Kira Hudson Banks, How Managers Can Promote Healthy Discussions About Race, HBR, January 2016.
[159] Carola Hoyos and Farva Kaukab, Should we focus more on race or less? Financial Times, May 2016.
[160] Chimamanda Ngozi Adiche, Americanah, Fourth State, 2013.
[161] https://implicit.harvard.edu/implicit/takeatest.html.

CHAPTER 11

[163] http://enar-eu.org/IMG/pdf/anti-semitism_briefing_2017.pdf
[163] https://www.eeoc.gov/eeoc/statistics/enforcement/religion.cfm.
[164] http://www.ukyouthparliament.org.uk/campaign/racism-and-religous-discrimination.
[165] Eurobarometer - Discrimination in the EU in 2015, European Commission, 2015.
[166] Pratiques religieuses en entreprise : Quelle réalité? Quelles remontées du terrain ? IMS – Charte de la Diversité, Septembre 2013.
[167] Eurobarometer - Discrimination in the EU in 2015, European Commission, 2015.

CHAPTER 12

[168] Managers Guide to LGBTI inclusion, Pride in Diversity, 2013.
[169] Managers Guide to LGBTI inclusion, Pride in Diversity, 2013.
[170] Stonewall, top 100 employers, 2016.
[171] http://www.vocativ.com/culture/lgbt/transgender-suicide/.
[172] Managers Guide to LGBTI inclusion, Pride in Diversity, 2013.
[173] Out in the world Infographic, Center for Talent Innovation, 2016.
[174] http://www.lawsociety.org.uk/support-services/advice/practice-notes/working-with-transgender-employees/.
[175] Managers Guide to LGBTI inclusion, Pride in Diversity, 2013.
[176] Stonewall, top 100 employers, 2016.

CHAPTER 13

[177] Global generations – a global study on work-life challenges across generations, EY, 2015.

[178] Guide du Manager de proximité, Observatoire de la parentalité, 2016.

[179] One In Five Americans Work From Home, Numbers Seen Rising Over 60 percent, Investing, 2013.

[180] Making flexible working work, Good Day at Work, 2016.

[181] Making flexible working work, Good Day at Work, 2016.

[182] Global generations – a global study on work-life challenges across generations, EY, 2015.

[183] One In Five Americans Work From Home, Numbers Seen Rising Over 60 percent, Investing, 2013.

[184] One In Five Americans Work From Home, Numbers Seen Rising Over 60 percent, Investing, 2013.

[185] Flexible working, making it work, Unison, 2014.

[186] Peter Hirst, How a Flex-Time Program at MIT Improved Productivity, Resilience, and Trust, HBR, June 2016.

[187] Flexible working, making it work, Unison, 2014.

[188] One In Five Americans Work From Home, Numbers Seen Rising Over 60 percent, Investing, 2013.

[189] Global generations – a global study on work-life challenges across generations, EY, 2015.

[190] Ron Eldrigde, Work/Life: A Balancing Act For Fathers Too, November 2016.

[191] http://www.acas.org.uk/index.aspx?articleid=1616

CONCLUSION

[192] Quote by Helio Rocha, one of Brazil's biggest digital marketing specialists.

[193] Tony Schwartz and Christine Porath, Your Boss's Work-Life Balance Matters as Much as Your Own, Harvard Business Review, July 2014.

Printed in Great Britain
by Amazon